MAGICAL ALBERT

*How a preemie foal changed one couple's
definition of family forever*

by Renata Lumsden

"*Magical Albert* is a rewarding account of harness racing and a couple's special horse... Lusi, Mach Magic, Magical Albert, and other horses are lovable within the text... The Lumsdens' personal experiences give the story depth...Albert stands out among their creatures: though he's deemed not likely to be a strong competitor because of the circumstances surrounding his birth, the Lumsdens choose to believe in him anyway. He and the other horses are shown to be a source of fulfillment and joy for the couple, becoming important members of the Lumsden family."

—*Foreward Clarion Reviews*

◆ FriesenPress

Suite 300 - 990 Fort St
Victoria, BC, V8V 3K2
Canada

www.friesenpress.com

In this memoir, the author has tried to recreate locales, events, and dialogue from her memories of them. The names and other identifying details of some minor characters have been changed to protect their privacy. The scenes in which the author is not present have been recreated through speaking with those who were, and occasionally, for the sake of narrative flow, events have been compressed.

Front Cover Photo and Back Cover Photo by Ranjit Singh

Author Photo by Norm Files

ISBN
978-1-5255-6931-9 (Hardcover)
978-1-5255-6932-6 (Paperback)
978-1-5255-6933-3 (eBook)

1. BIOGRAPHY & AUTOBIOGRAPHY, PERSONAL MEMOIRS

Distributed to the trade by The Ingram Book Company

For a lifetime of love, support, and encouragement,
I dedicate this book with endless gratitude to
my amazing mother, Eileen June Paulo.

Table of Contents

Introduction

The whole thing started way back with the decision of one man—a complete stranger to us—to breed his mare named Mollie Hanover with the illustrious Standardbred stallion Camluck.

In 2001 on February 9, while the cold winds howled in southwestern Ontario, Mollie gave birth to a filly. Inspired by a movie her owner had recently seen about magic, he chose the name Illusionist. He smiled when she stood and took her first steps to suckle at her mother's teat. Captivated by Illusionist's build and solid legs, her owner had high hopes for the foal.

As a two-year-old on the harness-racing circuit, Illusionist didn't disappoint. She performed very well, earning enough to make her attractive to other horsemen.

When Illusionist was three, she was sold. That's when she entered our lives. "Illusionist" was her racing name, although everyone called her Lusi—a short form of **Illusi**onist, but pronounced "Lucy." Initially my husband, Dave, brought her into our world with a partner. A year later, Dave saw her true character, speed, and potential, and he took over 100 percent of her reins as owner. Lusi's first winner's circle picture with us—along with all her other win photos and accomplishments—still hangs in the house today. As a couple, we directed all our emotional, financial, and physical efforts toward helping her become the best she could be while taking care to protect her health and emotional well-being.

Our close and rewarding relationship with Illusionist brought us unexpected gifts at all levels. Grateful that she was talented enough to earn over a million dollars racing, we retired our champion from the big oval in 2009 at the age of eight and vowed to keep her forever.

Five years later, with two foals behind her, I never dreamed Lusi's after-racing life as a broodmare would be anything but happy, healthy, and long. Nor did I or Dave suspect that an equine pregnancy gone sideways for Lusi and a heart-stopping birth for Albert, her premature foal, would test our commitment—to each other and the horses—in ways we'd never imagined.

That story is what formed the heart of my previous book, *The Bounty of Illusionist*. This book, *Magical Albert*, as its title suggests, has at its centre Albert, Lusi's preemie foal, who took us on a sometimes alarming, ultimately exhilarating, but always unpredictable journey, and who continues to impact our lives in often startling and wonderful ways.

To help you keep track of their lineage, below is a chart that includes some of the horses mentioned in this book and their dams and sires. Each horse below shares a common birthday on January first.[1]

---

1   Standardbred horse associations consider January 1 the "universal birthday" for all registered horses, rather than actual birth dates. This simplifies classifying horses by age. Note that Standardbred associations do not allow apostrophes in horses' registered names, but I've added them in the names He's Watching and She's Magic, and also included it in a few other names for readability.

Illusionist Parentage:

Illusionist Offspring:

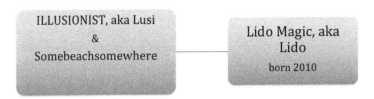

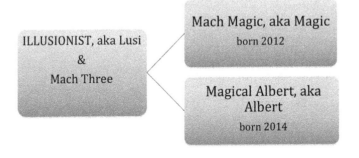

Illusionist Grandbabies:

Lido Magic
&
Sportswriter

Sarasota Magic, aka Sara
born 2014

Lido Magic
&
He's Watching

She's Magic, aka Sheshe
born 2017

Some Lucky Magic, aka Lucky
born 2018

Chapter 1

RISK AND REWARD

It was March 2014 and I'd taken a drive up to Hillsborough Stables with Dave. The equine maternity ward, better known as the foaling barn, sat between clumps of weathered old birch trees while the big main barn and training arena lay along a curved drive to the back. The buzz of anticipation was palpable. One of the resident mares was getting close— due even sooner than one of our own mares, Lido Magic.

Caregivers and midwives Darlene and Derrick Hayes had more than two decades of experience delivering foals. Hillsborough Stables was their pride-and-joy business. Light-hearted Derrick had deep blue eyes and a full-bodied voice that wrapped any listener, horses included, in an aura of tranquility. Blonde Darlene, known for her spirited laugh, zoomed through the barn day and night, keeping a careful eye on every horse, dog, and human. Her attention to detail was unparalleled as far as equine needs were concerned. Husband and wife treated each and every horse like a wonderful gift—pleasing owners like us—with no second-class citizens among the bunch. The pair knew Lusi and our small herd well.

Hillsborough Stables, where Lusi, her foals, and many other Standardbreds and Thoroughbreds lived, was tucked away in Millgrove, Ontario, about thirteen kilometres from the city of Hamilton. We pulled in and parked. Lusi's daughter Lido, due to foal in five weeks, gave us a welcome nicker of recognition from the paddock fence. Surrounded by her broodmare friends, Lido enjoyed a handful of sliced carrots Dave offered. Clutching another bag containing boxes of granola bars, I headed for the barn and the familiar last double stall on the left. My goal was to be the first to greet baby Albert and mother Lusi—before Dave did—and practice my horse-interaction skills.

Lusi's massive mature head and Albert's contrasting comical young face were framed through the opening in the stall door. Her face I knew so well. Lusi's irregularly shaped star had a cowlick at the base, and the white glow of the spot lit the depths of her eyes. Five years had passed since her retirement from the harness-racing circuit. She'd been at the centre of our equine family and lives for the past ten years. I couldn't imagine life without her now, or her babies.

Lusi, a granola-bar addict, heard me ruffle the plastic bag. She thrust her head through the stall-door opening. I peered inside as Albert moved back behind his mother's rump.

The whiteness of Lusi's girdle-shaped belly bandage shone sharply against her dark bay coat. Its sheer size, encircling her body pretty much from behind her withers to a few inches in front of her hips, had taken a while for me to adjust to. As an X-ray technologist, I was used to the scale of human medicine. I stared at the bandage and tried to imagine the length and depth of the hidden incision. I still couldn't quite believe that both mother Lusi and baby Albert had made it through an emergency Caesarean section.

Renata Lumsden

Two months earlier on January 6, just a couple of weeks before Lusi's foaling date, Darlene had noticed something off about the mare. Yes, she looked huge, but Darlene and Derrick knew she was prone to big babies. Typically, foals— male or female—weighed ninety to one hundred pounds at birth. Lusi's first two foals both weighed nearly 120 pounds, or about 54 kilograms; the couple had told Dave and me that they "both had to do some serious pulling" to get them out. But something else was going on; Lusi seemed listless. When Darlene took the horse's pulse and saw it was alarmingly high, she called the local vet, who advised trailering the mare immediately to the Ontario Veterinary College in Guelph, a half-hour from Millgrove. Our pacing champion had carefully hidden her pregnancy dilemma—a problem with her prepubic tendon and subsequent bowel herniation—until it was nearly too late.

At the college, the lead vet asked my husband a question no animal lover ever wanted to hear: "Who would you like us to save, the mare or the foal?"

Faced with this agonizing choice, Dave said, "Let's hope and pray that Lusi's baby pulls through, but the mare's the priority." I agreed. I had a bond with Lusi but none with her unborn foal, and anyway the odds were stacked against him. Unlike human infants, the vets told us, a foal delivered prematurely usually doesn't survive.

Upon hearing this, my scientific mind leaned toward a more compassionate ending—euthanasia. As a front-line healthcare worker who'd seen death up close, I shared my opinion with my husband.

"It seems the only right thing to do," I added. "We don't want the baby to suffer when he barely has a chance at life. "

Dave listened to me, and he listened to all the medical options offered by the vets. Albert had survived Lusi's C-section, but barely. (We'd chosen to keep the name

"Albert" offered by the vets at the hospital. It sounded noble, and began with the first letter of the alphabet, henceforth reminding us that our little fighter was the first foal born at the Ontario Veterinary College in 2014.) The newborn was exceptional in all that he was lacking. Still, Dave chose to give the vets the go-ahead to put Albert on a ventilator shortly after birth. The appliance artificially pumped oxygen into the baby's lungs and allowed carbon dioxide to escape. But I believed that the end lurked close by in Albert's case and that my husband was hiding behind a veil of ignorance.

Meanwhile, the hot shredded mess inside Lusi was carefully reconfigured. During the operation, the skilled surgeon did his best to mend all the grated tissue caused by Albert's substantial size. Only time would tell if Lusi would experience any future bowel herniation—often fatal in horses. Her odds of survival were pegged at a coin toss.

For his first ten days on earth, Albert did little else but lie on his side on a sheepskin blanket, and his bodily functions—poo, pee, eat, breathe—were delivered by a small army of machines, vets, and foal-watch volunteers. Besides having to be on the ventilator for nearly three days, the foal needed lube and water enemas to combat bowel obstruction, and the vets performed a small surgical adjustment to both of Albert's eyes to repair inward-folding eyelids. Normally, full-term foals were born with well-developed lung capacity; they quickly stood and nursed. Albert lacked the necessary muscle tone to even stand, and the pads of his feet were ominously dotted pink and bright red.

After each trek I made up to Guelph, my silent thoughts were clear and strong. If we didn't have to bury Albert the following week, then surely if he survived, he'd be partially blind and run in circles—if he could stand at all. Why were we taking on this impossible medical hurdle?

My scientific-based objections, when I did articulate them along the way, only increased Dave's devotion to the foal. He somehow put aside any negative ideas about Albert's future and didn't even try to gauge the benefits versus the costs involved. And the financial costs in the end were mind-boggling, I thought. But like a man faithfully standing by a long-time girlfriend, Dave took his responsibility seriously as the owner of a talented broodmare. Dave was devoted to Lusi. In his heart, the least he could do was try to save her only son.

But two months later, here was Albert, our miracle foal, standing, even running on his own now, and reunited with his mother, even if she couldn't nurse him.

"How's my girl?" I said to Lusi.

Her ears went back and she snaked her head in my direction. I never knew if I was in trouble or if she was only playing with me. Then she pressed her chest against the stall door, waiting. Her head was high, and she blew out a low nicker. I wished I spoke horse—I could never predict the outcome of a face-to-face meeting with Lusi. Reaching into the plastic bag, I ripped open the first box of peanut-butter granola bars. For a split second, I felt confused about how to proceed. Mingling with horses had never come naturally to me. Despite ten years of practice, I wasn't comfortable around the great beasts. Today as always, the peanut butter bar allowed me the close proximity I craved with her. I checked the position of Lusi's head in relation to my position, trying to imagine a horse's blind spot. *Never stand in the blind spot.* I shifted sideways, hoping to gain her approval.

The treat was in my hand. Lusi lowered her head until her whiskers tickled my palm. She found it. With powerful suction, Lusi inhaled her favourite snack. As the granola smell wafted through the air, Albert's nostrils flared and he craned his neck. I watched him. Like a colourful fishing float, he bobbed along behind his mom. Just then, the sound of laughing voices echoed from around the corner. Derrick, Darlene, and Dave burst down the shedrow toward me.

Married for nearly thirty years, Dave and I were well matched in more than a few ways. We had both been raised in middle-class fashion, but our families lived modestly. Growing up, there were no weekends or summers away at a lakeside cottage, no trips abroad, no horses or riding lessons. Dave and I had always loved animals, though, and he'd been exposed to harness racing at a young age through his father at Flamboro Downs in southern Ontario. So it wasn't a huge surprise that horses eventually came into our married lives, although our leap into Standardbred-horse ownership had only taken off within the last ten years. Nonetheless—big, bay, small, or grey—the horses had become a constant part of our lives.

Three decades ago, the closest I'd ever come to a Standardbred had been sitting beside Dave in the distant racetrack grandstands with a cold beer in one hand and a race program in the other. In the early days of our relationship, I remember Dave being thrilled that I was willing to include a night at the track on so many of our dates. The majestic competitors were long-bodied harness-racing horses, some-times called trotters and sometimes called pacers because of the different ways they moved their legs. Dave and I ate a lot of hamburgers and lost a few betting dollars. Other than that, my only encounters with racehorses involved seeing a long nose poking out the back window of a trailer as it sped along the highway toward distant competition, a sulky—a two-wheeled racing bike—strapped to the top.

Dave and I had met at university. Dave's business mind and education in economics combined with my healthcare-related education and my scientific approach to life had created much opportunity over the years for us to speak, listen, and be heard by one another. Dave was a great listener, but he didn't always take my advice. My listening skills were so-so.

Ever since we'd first met, Dave and I had hardly ever stopped talking. Well, maybe I did most of the talking. Perhaps because of my Italian heritage, I raised my voice sometimes and used my hands a lot. Dave, with his quiet Scottish manner, took in my squawks, appraised the situation, and then offered a different viewpoint that always made me stop and think. On our first date over dinner, we talked so much I hardly swallowed a bite. The cadence of his deep voice and his soft blue eyes had happily held me hostage.

Because of time spent at the track with his father, Dave had had far more exposure to the sport of harness racing than I had. Two decades into our marriage, he explained so persuasively that I had no choice but to agree with him: our owning two or three Standardbred horses was even better than owning one. But as it turned out, the purchase of Dave's first horse, in 2004, was a harbinger of things to come. In the years that have followed, my husband has owned many Standardbreds and together we've cheered on every mare, filly, colt, or gelding[2] that has graced the barn and our lives, though Lusi held pride of place in our herd. A champion like her didn't come along every day. We knew how special she was, and how rare. As far as I was concerned, she deserved all the treats in the world.

After snatching the granola bar out of my hand, Lusi moved back into the stall. I was sure the enthusiastic

---

2   A gelding is a castrated horse. Diminished hormone levels are said to calm the horse.

crunching sounds she made could be heard throughout the barn. Albert watched and listened.

"Here," I said to Dave, who was now standing beside me. I dropped some granola-bar pieces into his cupped hand.

Lusi jammed her head through the opening with eyes big and wide and ears cranked forward. Her nose hovered right beside Dave's face, and she let him kiss her muzzle as he fed her. While I constantly walked a tightrope with Lusi trying to prove myself to her, literally not knowing sometimes whether to advance or retreat in her presence—one momentary lapse in focus or judgment, and I felt she might bite my finger or kick at my kneecaps—Lusi never pinned her ears back for Dave or gave him attitude. She seemed to like men.

Bits of granola crumbs stuck to Lusi's whiskers. Her long pink tongue whipped in and out so energetically I feared Dave might get wet-kissed on the lips. Satisfied, Lusi shifted back and stood mid-stall. I stayed stock-still at the stall door, trying not to stare at Albert but wishing the youngster would move in my direction.

Then it happened. Albert shifted one leg in front of the other until his nose burst through the stall opening.

"Hi, Albert," Dave and I chimed at the same time.

The foal's ears pricked, and he moved another step closer.

Albert and I stood head to head while the others chatted. The foal's nostrils flared; he was taking in my scent. Without warning, his whiskers tickled my cheek. I reached out and brushed his mane and neck with my nervous fingers. I inhaled the colt's fragrant smell and felt myself grow calmer. Face to face, Albert and I became locked in a silent, intimate exchange. The kindness in the depths of his expressive gaze signalled the beginning of a friendship. I traced his entire body with my eyes, memorizing each contour and change in shading from head to toe. In the stillness of that moment,

I felt fully present. Little did I know the effect the young horse's spirit would have on me or us in the future.

Out of the corner of my eye, I noticed Dave and Darlene watching me. Derrick was nowhere in sight. I straightened my posture and took a deep breath. Albert stayed put.

Suddenly I heard Derrick shout, "It's feeding time! It's feeding time," as he hurried down the shedrow carrying a steaming blue bucket of mares' milk replacer. Albert quickly shuffled and moved over near the sliding door. Lusi retreated farther back into the stall.

"Who wants to feed Albert?" Derrick said.

I stumbled, unsure. "Let Dave," I said.

Dave grabbed my arm and nudged me into the stall. "You go, Renata. I'll record a video."

My goodness! It was all I could do to rein in my excitement for fear of upsetting Albert at mealtime.

Albert was watchful, but I sensed he was more curious than afraid. I stepped forward, which brought me within inches of him.

Derrick came in behind me. He and Darlene were having a hard time remembering what life had been like without the responsibility of Albert's hourly feedings. With the bucket in hand, Derrick offered me a quick foal-feeding tutorial.

"Hold the bucket. Now when Albert gets to the bottom, he'll knock it with his head." Derrick handed me the steaming hot pail. "I'm warning you, make sure you've still got a good tight hold of the bucket." He chuckled.

The milk bubbled and swished creamy white against the blue bucket. Albert lowered his head and started drinking. Thrilled to be so close to the latest addition to our equine family, I was so zoned into Albert's feeding that everything moved in slow motion. Albert sucked and the level of the liquid lowered. The horse's delicate, pointy ears were so close to my chin, I could almost plant a kiss on both.[3] "I'm so thankful you're here with us today," I whispered.

Nicker. Nicker. Less than a foot away, Lusi's dark eyes, soft with their fierce love for her young son, watched. Lusi, a mother of two beautiful fillies previously, had surprised us all with her recent pregnancy predicament and victory against the claws of death. Albert's arrival marked her third foal. But sadly, he would be her last.

3   **Renata Lumsden** , *The Bounty of Illusionist: Hillsborough* (Victoria, BC: FriesenPress, 2017), 214–17.

Chapter 2

FEAST AND FAMINE

That night I hardly slept. Dave's rhythmic breathing beside me held my attention. Too excited from the farm visit earlier and even more excited about the gathering the next day, I limited my tossing and turning so that only one of us would be sleep-deprived. I'd been the same way as a child—celebrations always turned me into a tight ball of nervous anticipation. And we had a great deal to celebrate.

The following evening, the last light of dusk barely lit the spring sky. Tucked away in an unassuming strip mall in Burlington, a city at the northwestern end of Lake Ontario, the windowless restaurant sat among a hair salon, a coin-operated laundromat, and a variety store. The steakhouse attracted visitors from as far away as Nova Scotia and Vancouver, and its aged mouth-watering cuts, fresh seafood, and steaming baked potatoes were befitting of a retired mare's accomplishments. Dave arranged a celebratory ritual at this restaurant each time Lusi gave birth. The gathering allowed us to pause and give thanks for what we called "the bounty of Illusionist."

The group of invitees had somehow managed to coordinate their hectic schedules. From one year to the next, the date for the dinner always seemed to fall sometime during the height of foaling season. Lusi and Albert had led the foaling parade at Hillsborough Stables a few months earlier in January. Coming out of that tough tunnel now in March, with mare and foal healthy and safe, had softened things, although the memories of those agonizing weeks at the veterinary hospital were still strong. The outcome could have been drastically different.

As we sat there in the restaurant with key players in the Lusi-and-Albert adventure, it all seemed like a giant dream come true.

Derrick and Darlene smiled at me across the table. Their ever-present beeper sat between their dinner plates, and I could tell that sleep deprivation was nibbling away at the equine—midwife couple. But the blend of enthusiastic voices, clattering cutlery on china plates, and the chance to step outside into the cool night air from time to time seemed to make it easier for them to stay awake.

Standardbred-horse trainer Travis Umphrey had joined the party again. The birth of Lusi's first son surprised everyone connected to the mare, including Travis, who had been charged with training Lusi's previous two fillies: four-year-old Lido Magic, due to foal soon herself, and her little sister, two-year-old Mach Magic. Travis loved harness racing thanks to a deep family history in the sport. The young trainer learned as he went from everyone around him, including his grandfather and everyone else he worked for and with over the years.

First-timers to the celebration, Dr. Luis Arroyo and his wife, Nicola, rounded out the guest list. Dr. Arroyo was the veterinarian who'd examined Lusi that cold January afternoon, ordered the emergency C-section, and helped assemble a team of reproductive specialists. The mare's recovery and Albert's preemie care remained in Dr. Arroyo's hands until both animals went home. Nicola was also a veterinarian, and she too worked and taught at the Ontario Veterinary College.

Conversation flowed. Old friendships were tightened and new friendships cast on. Love of horses was the common thread that bound us and made things easy and light. During the meal, I rose with my glass of red wine in the air. "To Albert and Lusi," I said. The sharp ringing sound of crystal clinking in unison filled the air. I kept the floor and added, "To my husband. Only Dave Lumsden would put a foal with little or no chance of surviving on a ventilator."

"Thank goodness he did," Derrick said. The bright smile across his wind-burnt face lit up the horseman's eyes.

"Cheers to that," I said, lifting my glass higher in the air. The group's voices rose.

"Albert threw a curve at every turn," Dr. Arroyo said. Although he sat with military posture, the vet's dark brown eyes were soft and empathetic. "The ventilator. Bowel obstruction. Feeding tubes. Those medical decisions must have been hard on you both."

"Well…" Dave said. He turned and looked at me with eyebrows raised.

I'd seen that look before. "It was tough, all right," I said. The time for me to confess had arrived. I stared at the vet and then took a quick sip of water. "At one point, I swore that if Albert lived—and Lusi, for that matter, after the C-section—then I'd need to re-evaluate my perspective on life and my approach to all major decisions." Feeling dry in the mouth, I took another sip. "I was that certain things would end badly, especially for Albert."

The vet's head shifted back. He blinked repeatedly, as if my blunt honesty had taken him by surprise. His wife studied me. After a few quiet seconds, Dr. Arroyo recovered. "Well, Renata. Lusi and Albert beat the odds." He grinned.

I grabbed my wine glass and downed more than a mouthful. "They certainly did."

"So, how goes it?" Dr. Arroyo said.

"Goes what?" I said.

"Your new approach to major decisions?" The vet's eyes shifted between Dave and me.

"Oh, that." I took a deep breath. "So... before Albert's arrival, I'd always taken a purely logical approach and measured things against a list of scientific pros and cons." I took another deep breath. "Now I listen with more empathy, and I force myself to see alternatives, even if the odds are slim."

Dr. Arroyo smiled. "Is it working?"

"Well... it comes and goes. After all, it's a newly acquired skill." I swallowed the lump in my throat. "Dave's a special man. I'm glad he proved me wrong, and that both horses made it." I turned and gave Dave a wink.

Standing outside in front of the restaurant, Dave and I waved and watched the glow of the taillights dull and shrink when the last guest drove away. As we pulled out of Burlington, I couldn't help but recall the past with Dave and roll over in my mind the night's events and our ties to the horses. Zooming along the Queen Elizabeth Highway, we held hands but didn't speak. Silence with this man I'd known for almost thirty years never felt uncomfortable.

Our return in 2014 from the greater Toronto area to this part of the world felt as cozy as slipping back into a well-worn cardigan. A short drive from Burlington, our Cape-Cod-style home in picturesque Ancaster held all the peace and quiet anyone could wish for. Situated between the big-city bustle of Toronto and the tourist town of Niagara Falls, little Ancaster sat up high on a vast limestone formation. More than a decade earlier, Ancaster's community had amalgamated with the larger city of Hamilton, which we knew well from our days at university.

During the drive home up the Hamilton Mountain with my stomach full and my face tired from laughing and talking, I felt alive and grateful as the fresh air from the slightly open car window brushed my face.

Once settled at home, Dave and I exchanged details lost during dinner amid the clamour of simultaneous conversations going on within our group.

"Hillsborough Stables needs our help," Dave said. He barked the message from the hallway walk-in closet.

"Help? What do you mean?" I replied from the bedroom.

"It's related to the government's decisions."

"The government?" My mind had trouble shifting gears.

"Remember? The province withdrew support for horse racing two years ago," Dave said. "Since then, the industry's taken a hit." We knew—and had been forcefully reminded by Lusi and Albert—that the horse world was unpredictable. In this case, an unpredictable government had made it more so.

In 1998, the Ontario government was looking for new revenue streams and developed a program called Slots at Racetracks Program (SARP). Finding a home beside racetracks for the slot machines required buy-in. So the tracks added one-armed bandits to their operations and got to keep a modest 20 percent of the take—the government got the remainder—resulting in incentives for horse trainers and horse owners in the form of higher race purses.

But SARP was suddenly cancelled in 2012, for reasons that later appeared to be short-sighted and ill-advised. The dissolution of the program left horse-racing personnel, equine industries, and rural small towns in the province hanging in the balance. The loss of the slots revenue hurt the racetrack purse structure, and racing at all levels suffered a blow. In Ontario, stallions standing at stud and the number of mares bred annually fell dramatically; yearling sales suffered as a result. The number of farms that went up for sale shocked me. With no new horse owners in sight and long-time owners like Dave and me paring down, opportunities to train and race in Ontario almost dried up.

I and many others wrote to the government-appointed ombudsman in the hopes of encouraging a restart. Instead, some racetracks shut down and the government threatened to pull the slots in others. Stories spread fast about horses being euthanized simply because cash-strapped owners couldn't afford to keep them. Horse owners likened it to deciding which child to sell to make ends meet for the rest of the family. Too many horses ended up at the end of the line.

The horses, with their heads held high and proud, had done nothing wrong. They were sentenced and punished. Fillies, fertile mares, fine colts, and fast geldings—the lucky ones—got a stay of execution, albeit without a guaranteed positive outcome, while others received an immediate death sentence. The value of horses remaining in Ontario fell drastically. Horse people who purchased animals from cash-strapped owners and intended to ride out the calamity only delayed the inevitable for some animals. It all seemed very sad and unnecessary to Dave and me.

With the 2013 change in leadership at the provincial level, however, negotiations between key players, coupled with outcries from individuals, seemed to shelve blame and instead attempted to resolve issues. But SARP remained cancelled, and while some in the racing industry took tentative steps forward in the new landscape, others could never, and would never, fully recover.

"So purse payouts are really down," Dave explained, "but farm rental, horse feed, training, and vet bills all still cost the same." The math was easy: fewer horses and less money coming in through race purses, but the same fee schedules. Until tonight, though, I'd had no idea how badly the backlash from the government had affected our friends at Hillsborough Stables and our own small herd.

"Darlene mentioned foaling numbers," I said. I switched off the bathroom light.

"Right. The drop in the number of mares in foal has taken a chunk out of Hillsborough's usual breeding and broodmare revenue." Dave, now in his pyjamas, sat down on the bench at the end of the bed. "Horse owners, just like us, have sold horses. Other owners have moved animals across the border to race. Either way, there are fewer around."

"Hmm…" I nestled down beside him. "We're down to one racehorse. Just Mach Magic."

"Down from five to one," Dave said. He gave me a half grin.

I nodded. "I get it—the math makes sense."

In the past, when we had more horses, we raced more often and won more high-calibre competitions with bigger purses. We hadn't had a champion like Lusi since she'd retired in 2009. Having been involved in this industry for more than a decade, I knew fates could turn quickly, but things had never before sounded this cruel. We were hardly alone in feeling the squeeze in the horse business, but we were at least fortunate that our primary income came from solid sources outside of racing. So many folks who were invested solely in harness racing—both personally and professionally—were trying to sell horses to other people in Ontario who couldn't afford to take them. In short, horse people had literally bet their farms and were on the brink of possibly losing them.

"Hillsborough Stables is still home to Lido, Lusi, and Albert," I said. Mach Magic was training at Travis's stable.

"But Derrick and Darlene's lease is nearly ten years old—they're not earning the same now to justify the rent they're paying."

I felt my heart sink. Dave put his hand on my knee and squeezed. "There's more," he said.

The tone of his voice made me brace myself. I looked up at him. "What else?"

"Travis wants out of the horse business."

"What?" I couldn't seem to quite take in what he was saying. "You're sure?"

Dave's patient gaze told me that he understood my confusion. "Travis can't make a go of it anymore. He's short horses."

With too few horses to make ends meet, Travis planned to move his small stable, including our mare, Mach Magic, to a mutual friend and respected horse trainer named Ted MacDonnell.

"Wow." Robotically, I closed the bedroom door.

"Travis needs a regular job." Dave said. He folded down the bedcovers. "He needs a steady income."

"You mean outside of harness racing?" For the first time since we'd started talking, the room felt cold. I crawled beneath the warmth of the covers and slid closer to Dave's side of the bed.

"Yes." Dave put his arm around me. "If Travis gets his AZ licence, then I can offer him a job. We're always looking for truck drivers at the Hamilton concrete plant." He let out a heavy sigh. "It is what it is, Renata. Travis needs a hand. He's a hard worker and a nice guy."

I stayed quiet, digesting this new reality. With my ear against Dave's chest, I could hear the faint drumbeat of his heart.

Renata Lumsden

"Darlene and Derrick asked me to help them look for a farm," Dave said. "Their lease is up November thirtieth, and—"

"A farm?" I interrupted. "What if they don't find anything suitable?"

"Once the weather gets warmer, we'll see what's out there."

"Hillsborough Stables? The horses? Our horses? They're all going to move?" I said, trying to keep up.

"Derrick, Darlene, and the horses need to get out of there, and soon," Dave said. I noted the determined edge in his voice. He rolled over and turned out the bedside light.

I had no idea this political and financial dilemma had hit us so close to home. As I pondered all this new information about Travis, Hillsborough Stables, our horses, and harness racing, I felt grateful that we were able to maintain our modest numbers of equine mouths to feed despite the situation. Mach Magic was the only horse we had floating around the big oval these days. But even if she won every competition—which wasn't realistic—she couldn't carry the expenses of our tiny herd on her back. Mach Magic was good, but she was no Lusi.

The future for our horses looked bleak. The one bright spot in all this was the impending birth of Lido's foal. Maybe, I thought, this little one, who carried the genes of two great pacers, Lusi and Sportswriter, would become another champion.

But life can change in a heartbeat, and the unpredictable was about to rear up once again.

Chapter 3

THE UNEXPECTED

In the end, Lusi's first born, Lido Magic, never raced.

It had taken sometime for Dave and me to name her. We chose "Magic" after the name Illusionist. Lido, as she's called for short, means "beach" in Italian, and was inspired by her sire, Somebeachsomewhere, as well as by Lido Key in Sarasota, Florida, where we'd taken long walks and enjoyed breathtaking sunsets.

In 2010, the day after Lido was born, we raced up to Hillsborough Stables. Dave and I couldn't wait to lay our eyes on the baby and praise Lusi for a job well done. It was our first experience with foals. While I'd suggested we attend the actual birthing event, Dave thought we'd only be in the way. After Lusi delivered Lido, we met Darlene and Derrick in the foaling barn, and some of the staff also joined us at the stall threshold. The sight of the sweet newborn foal elicited the kind of awed sounds reserved for pyrotechnic competitions involving fireworks on Canada Day.[4]

---

4 **Renata Lumsden**, *The Bounty of Illusionist: Broodmare* (Victoria, BC: FriesenPress, 2017), 64–67.

Lido was a big strong foal with a Roman nose and a white star, and she had plenty of bone. At the time Dave had said, "With her breeding and build, she looks like a winner."

When she was two, we sent her to Travis for training, but a few months later Lido suffered a bout of colic—sometimes fatal in horses. She avoided surgery for the condition, which in her case involved a twisted bowel, and after making what looked like a full recovery, Lido got back to learning her sport. Everyone kept an eye on her well-being and her timed miles, knowing that a one-second fraction in the sport was equal to five horse lengths. Or simply put, one fifth of a second was equal to a single horse length.

Lido looked good in her schooling races with other newbies. Balanced and well gaited, she paced behind the starting gate with other fillies her age. However, although born with natural skills and instincts, the mare lacked enthusiasm despite the added competition around her, going a slow 2:05 seconds each time, which translated into nearly twenty-five horse lengths behind competitors racing at or near the two-minute mark. During training-mile workouts, meant to build muscle strength and decrease timed quarter fractions, she responded in ways that left us wondering about her overall interest in the sport for which she'd been bred. Instead of heeding Travis's command to go faster, Lido slowed and tried to kick the nuisance trainer in the jog cart. We all thought that perhaps the colic episode had soured her on racing.

Lido might have made it to the track with some stronger urging; instead Dave chose another route. He noted that she was tall like Lusi, with muscles woven around strong bones and a not-so-small bottom. Lido's build and bloodlines, especially through her sire Somebeachsomewhere, made her more than suitable for a broodmare career.

Now in 2014, at age four and in foal with her first baby, Lido Magic glowed. She was the picture of broodmare health. And according to Darlene, she'd established herself as something of a prima donna, just like her mother, Lusi, sometimes taking charge among the broodmare group.

At less than one week away, Lido's due date was fast approaching. I knew horses didn't need help to bring new life to earth, but the eyes and hands of the midwives at the stables helped settle my nervous stomach.

Darlene and Derrick's profession was not one for the snobbish. Rarely captured in a race-win photo due to their unpredictable and demanding schedules—foaling, feeding, mucking stalls, tending to post-surgical or sick horses—the couple kept watch over nearly sixty acres and more than three dozen animals. Some were there for rest and time off from racing, others for surgical recovery. And then, of course, there were the broodmares—though fewer that year than in the past. In rubber boots and cotton Keeneland sweatshirts zipped to the neck, Darlene and Derrick were rewarded time and again by the whinny of a group of hungry broodmares at feeding time or by eye contact with some relaxed competitors before they rushed to the nightly hay.

Anticipation and excitement hung in the air for Dave and me. In our horse history, we'd never before welcomed the arrival of more than one foal per year. Lusi and her son Albert were doing well, and soon another baby would join our small herd. A yellowish wax had recently appeared on the end of the young mother-to-be's teats, which signalled milk secretion and that Lido had "bagged up"—a term used by horse folk to describe the broodmare's development of an udder.

The waxing of the horse's teats signalled to the midwives that Lido was getting close. They brought her inside. Darlene washed down her body and braided the upper half of her tail. All signs and preparation for the impending delivery had aligned on schedule, and things seemed to be progressing well.

Suddenly, everything changed.

It was late. Dave was looking somewhat confused when he came upstairs from the basement on his way to bed. "What is it?" I said.

"Darlene called. Lido is having the baby." Dave's blue eyes held my attention. He should have sounded happy, I thought, but his tone didn't match his words.

"What's wrong?" I said.

Dave grabbed my hand. "Sit down, Renata."

His strained look really had me worried. Owning Standardbred horses had always presented some ups and downs, but the broodmares, like Lusi and Lido, held a special spot in my heart. "What's wrong?" I repeated. For a moment I could feel myself stop breathing.

"There's a problem," Dave said. "It's a red-bag delivery." His words hung in the air for a few seconds.

My inner voice immediately reacted, saying, "*Big trouble!*" With the blood-filled placenta detached from the uterus, it meant the unborn foal no longer received oxygen through its umbilical cord. I knew the baby would crave air on its way through the birthing canal. Imagining the foal inhaling in an air-tight space, I felt sick inside. Time was short.

Dave and I paced and waited.

Finally, the call came from Hillsborough Stables. It was a classic red-bag delivery, according to Darlene—one she'd seen more than a few times in her career. In graphic detail, which left Dave's face white, the midwife told us that because the placenta was emerging first, they'd had to cut it open and then reach in to break the white amniotic sac around the foal.

I maintained a poker face. Yet inside, I couldn't shake the feeling that we were in a bad spot on this one. With a professional background in health care, I'd seen enough human deliveries gone badly, both for the mothers and their newborn babies. I tried to picture the placenta bulge and Derrick and Darlene's reaction. I could see them blinking rapidly at first as they sprang into action, then working to get the foal out fast. The odd order of events for Lido and her placenta made me say a silent prayer.

Dave and I knew from past encounters that a healthy foal was the result of good prenatal practices, genetics, and some luck. Conception started in the least romantic way, by artificial insemination. Breeders, like us, carefully scrutinized potential genetic crosses between their mares and various sire candidates to stay clear of inbreeding. Then diet, dental care, parasite control, vaccinations, stall rental, and turnout time for the broodmare to exercise at will required a financial commitment approximately equal to the cost of buying a ten-year-old pickup truck, or $8,000 per year.

We'd thought we'd seen and heard it all with Lusi and the delivery of her three previous foals, but Lido took a different approach in the delivery stall. We'd seen our horses sleep standing up and lying down, but we had no idea broodmares could have babies in either position. According to Darlene, even in a typical delivery, the mare stands, rolls, and may lie down more than once in an effort to coax the baby into the proper position to enter the world. Most mares went down on the stall floor during the delivery; however, some, like Lido, insisted on standing.

Lido's position allowed gravity to help bring the foal out faster. The mare's uterus contracted gently and hastily. With two pairs of hands, Derrick and Darlene assisted the first-time mom by swiftly directing the baby into the world.

The eleven-month gestation for our unraced mare Lido Magic ended at 1:00 a.m. on April 8. Lusi became a grandmother. The Chinese Year of the Horse, 2014, had brought us Albert in January and now a sweet filly.

Dave and I were relieved when the pictures finally popped up on the cell phone. Lido's long neck was slung down toward the baby—her giant head hovering above the newborn's ears.

Darlene told us the mare made quiet vocalizations during the cleaning process. Lido began licking at the foal's head. By the time she reached the baby's rump, the new mom had gently helped the filly with standing. Erect and proud, the newborn stood with her eyes on the camera. The youngster's white star shone bright above her deep chocolate eyes. Under the evening stall lights, the less-than-one-hour-old baby looked petite, but she was a good weight at just over ninety pounds, according to reports from Hillsborough.

More images bubbled up. In one picture, Derrick beamed as he knelt inside the stall door, the baby's nose nearly touching his.

"Lido's first baby," Dave said, his eyes glued to his phone.

Together we watched a short video clip Darlene had sent. The baby scampered unsteadily at first and then found her way to Lido's teat. The foal pulled and suckled. Lido didn't even raise a leg in protest.

"And to think it was only four years ago that Lusi delivered Lido," I said.

Dave took my hand, smiled, and nodded, acknowledging the fact that Illusionist's bounty within our horse family had taken another leap forward.

The next day after work, Dave and I sat around the dinner table thinking about a winning horse name. Obeying the criteria of no more than eighteen characters and four words, the foal's forever name needed to sound good when blared through racetrack loudspeakers. Dave went down to the basement and came back with a bottle in hand. He popped the cork and sniffed, then poured. We raised our glasses of wine and toasted. "To Lido, the baby, and grandmother Lusi," Dave said.

"Cheers!" I set down my glass and picked up two plates of steaming pasta heaped with red sauce and giant meatballs. Dave's favourite meal was my "go to" during celebrations.

Naming horse-babies was a ritual for us: Lusi's three foals, and now Lido's first. According to regulations at Standardbred Canada, the designation had to be submitted within the first year of the baby's life. In the past, we'd agonized over the task of naming foals, and were often late picking the name and even later submitting the formal paperwork. Acceptance or rejection of the moniker was based on a number of intricate details and history. We'd never had a name rejected, so although slow, we were careful.

"Well," Dave began, "let's look at the sire and grandsire for starters."

The new foal's sire was Sportswriter, but her grandfather was Somebeachsomewhere.

"We can't forget Illusionist," I said between mouthfuls.

Dave grabbed a pencil and pad of paper. "Let's keep the name Magic in there for a subtle reference to Illusionist, and Lusi's racing name."

"Yes, I like that."

"Picking these is tough," he said, then swirled some pasta onto his fork.

Only the clinking of cutlery on stoneware plates could be heard as we considered options.

"Sarasota Magic," I said. It sounded like a winner to me.

"Sarasota in Florida, and Magic," Dave said. He scribbled the name on the page. "You may have something there."

"Lusi's covered," I said. "And there's a hint of the beach on Lido Key."

"Yes." Dave nodded. "You've included the grandsire that way with a nod to Somebeachsomewhere." He added a check mark.

Informally, we'd christened Lido's filly Sarasota Magic. The name would sound unique, we thought, bellowed around the racetrack. It would be shortened to Sara in the stable. All our horses had racing names and barn names— Illusionist was Lusi, Lido Magic was Lido, and Mach Magic was Magic, while Albert had yet to be given an official racing name. (We'd crafted a list of contenders, but none that Dave or I could agree upon.)

I jumped up and grabbed my phone. My fingers flew across the keyboard as I texted the name Sarasota Magic to Darlene and Derrick.

"I think they'll like it," Dave said.

I took a sip of wine. "Hope so."

A light breeze blew in from the slightly ajar patio door. One of our two cats, chubby black-and-white Martha, sat with her ear pressed up against the screen, listening to the loud chatter from blue jays in a nearby honey-locust tree. The other cat, a tabby named Joy, crouched a few feet away, staring up at the branches.

Bing! Bing! I looked down at my phone. The new text from Darlene responded with a single thumbs-up sign. It was official: Sarasota Magic—Sara for short.

I took a box of Italian treats from the fridge. "We have to get up there soon," I said.

Dave grabbed a pastry. "We'll go to Hillsborough this weekend." Suddenly the cream from the cannoli in his hand squirted out the back end. We laughed.

Bing! Bing! Now it was photos popping up. Mother Lido was resting her muzzle on Sara's neck while the baby lay motionless on a bed of hay in what looked like a deep slumber. I crossed my fingers, hoping this little filly would be healthy and bypass any challenges like those we'd seen with Albert a few months earlier. I couldn't wait to meet Sara in person and also stroke Albert's forelock and mane again.

Chapter 4

READ ALL ABOUT IT

Meanwhile, word of Lusi and Albert's unique medical adventure in Guelph had spread throughout the Standardbred community. A month earlier, in March, the story of Lusi, Albert, and the emergency C-section had made front-page news in a prominent Canadian harness-racing publication, *Trot Magazine*.

The six-page article was titled "Miracle—How a mother and her foal defied the odds." In glossy front-page colour, Darlene stood between the pair of horses, feeding Lusi what else but a peanut-butter-bar treat. Illusionist's magnificent head stood out in the foreground; our mare held her muzzle close to her son's, and her deep brown eyes focused on her foal, who gazed back at her. Compared to his mom's, Albert's head looked small and frail. His hairless spots, from bedsores and needles, were in full view, especially where various lifesaving lines of plastic tubing had been held in place.

With a variety of interior photos, the article captured Albert on the ventilator, the in-hospital reunion between mare and foal weeks after surgery, and the happy ending when both horses finally left the vet hospital and went home to Hillsborough Stables.

April morning, nearly a month after the article in *Trot Magazine*, I lay quiet a moment gathering my wits. It wasn't a typical Wednesday. I shot out of bed and woke Dave in the process. It was later than I thought, and today was the reunion.

"*The Toronto Star*," I mumbled to Dave with my toothbrush sticking out sideways.

"That's today?" Dave sat up.

Word was getting around about the case that had had vets up in Guelph working overtime, the unusual choice by owner Dave to save his mare, and the lucky premature foal that also survived. I knew that Dave's determination to save the foal as well as the mare was unconventional. In the racing world most would—I suspect—have put the time and funds into saving the foal, because if Lusi survived, her days as a broodmare would be over. The vets suggested mind-boggling and elaborate alternatives, such as cultivating her eggs and using a surrogate mare. Otherwise, she'd become a pasture horse, or what some might call an expensive lawn ornament. Many horse people would have considered Albert's unknown potential as a racehorse the sole upside. Dave's focus, however, on saving Lusi was the one clear objective that I'd wholeheartedly agreed with. Whatever motives guided his decision-making, they worked, since both mare and foal survived.

"They're sending two guys," I said. We'd organized a reunion, at the newspaper's request, of those involved in the story. Everyone was scheduled to arrive at 10:00 a.m.

I left ahead of Dave. It was warmer than usual for that time of year; nature had slept and died during the long cold winter, but had awakened now full of life and renewed energy. I practised mindfulness during the forty-minute drive and took in the floating white clouds and brown farmer's fields. I was proud as hell about showcasing mother Lusi and her miracle foal. I did my best to squash any doubtful thoughts about Albert's racing future. "Live in the moment," I told myself.

For Darlene and Derrick, who arose before dawn, it had already been a full morning. The midwives had told us they were more than happy to answer questions and parade the horses, provided it didn't interfere too much with their routine.

Pulling through the wrought-iron gates, I noticed a cameraman setting up his equipment not far from the board-and-batten house, while Darlene had the attention of a second man in the driveway. Tall and lean, with a pad of paper and pen in hand, at times he'd pull out his cell phone, which I assumed he was using to record her information.

Dave showed up about fifteen minutes after I did. "The folks from Guelph are a little lost," he said.

"Lost?" This was the vets' first trip to Hillsborough Stables. "All the concession roads and township lines of Millgrove must have gotten them confused."

"I think I got them straightened around," Dave said.

A moment later, the vets pulled in. Dr. Arroyo smiled from behind the steering wheel. The mid-size car was nearly full; two graduate students who'd been charged with Lusi and Albert's care had come along. Now the interview could really begin.

Lusi and Albert were waiting in the big broodmare stall up ahead.

"Morning, Lusi!" Darlene shouted from the shedrow before she dived into the stall.

I watched. Lusi stopped grazing on her hay and thrust her head through the V-shaped opening between the bars. In fact, every head down the shedrow jerked high, including

Albert's beside her. A half-dozen pairs of pointed ears poked out from the stalls, as if all the residents wanted to check out the newcomers.

Derrick and Darlene led Albert and Lusi outside, where the small crowd had gathered. It took a few moments for Derrick to get the silly-legged youngster to settle. Posing on the asphalt drive between the foaling barn and arena, Albert seemed confused. I suspected it was because he didn't know why his handlers were stopping instead of heading straight to the open arena for his usual morning exercise. Mother Lusi stood still while chickadees and barn swallows flew about, adding to the visual harmony of the healthy bay mare and her sturdy bay foal. The sky, a patchwork of blue and white, provided the perfect backdrop.

Bobbing and twisting, Albert was energetic and lively. At barely three months old and weighing more than three hundred pounds, he was undeniably huge. Beside him, her eyes liquid and large, Lusi seemed to exude confidence and pride. Our retired champion took the media attention in stride. Without looking like she gave it a second thought—the winner's circle stance now came naturally—she posed for the newspaper photos.

On cue, Derrick and Darlene led both horses inside and down the shedrow. With his tail flying behind him, Albert burst into the fenced-off enclosure within the arena and took off, throwing in the occasional buck. Oscar, the boxer farm dog, barked each time the foal's back legs shot up into the air. Meanwhile, a farmhand led Lusi around the indoor area to stretch her legs, her belly bandage intact. Her time to run and buck would come when she was fully healed.

After more than a dozen photo sessions inside and out, the reporter made his rounds. His calm, low voice, coupled with his relaxed manner, seemed to put the group at ease. Everyone, including the veterinarians, spoke as if they were talking directly to the reader, I thought—not through the filter of the reporter—as they filled in the who, what, where, why, and when of Albert and Lusi's beautiful story.

I slipped quietly into the background and listened. One consistent theme prevailed in each version regardless of the narrator: the horses were living beings that deserved patience and care. And because of Dave's faith and commitment, along with the special skills of the veterinarians at Guelph, Albert and Lusi had both survived. The unlikely outcome for the foal had revealed a "Magical Albert"—the racing name we finally settled on—all thanks to Dave's dedication.

Later, the photographer took us aside. "I'd like to create a video rendition of the story—a synopsis—to accompany the written piece," he said, waving his video camera in the air.

Dave motioned to me. "Go for it."

I shook my head. "If it weren't for you, Albert wouldn't be here, and none of this would have happened." I grinned and gave Dave a quick peck on the cheek.

"Are you sure?" Dave's eyes were locked on mine.

Dave's role in Lusi and Albert's tale made him the obvious choice, but I also reminded him that my tin voice and occasional lisp were less than appealing. He laughed. I squeezed Dave's hand and sent him and the photographer down the shedrow to the double stall. I followed and stood watching from a safe—in terms of distraction—distance.

Now back from the arena, both horses stood mid-stall. Lusi was her usual aloof self during the video, head down, snacking on hay. Albert caught Dave's voice and peered through the bars with eyes wide and ears forward, as if he didn't want to be left out.

Dave held the iron stall bars with one hand and spoke to the camera. His five fingers sat within reach of Albert. The foal moved closer. A few minutes passed. Suddenly Dave yanked his hand away. "Ouch! Why are you biting me?" he exclaimed. The reporter must have decided that moment was an amusing place to end the interview, because the red camera light went dark.

Dave shoved both hands into his jacket pockets and stared at Albert. With nostrils flared, the foal thrust his nose through the half stall door. Dave produced a small carrot and Albert tried to squeeze even closer.

"Oh. Now you want to be my friend," Dave said. "You want this?" He broke and bit the carrot into smaller, foal-size pieces and offered them to Albert, lovingly scratching the foal's neck as he ate. Lusi paid little or no attention. She had caught the scent of peanut butter bars being offered from the opposite stall entrance, where a group had recently gathered.

Following the video recording, Dave and I checked in on Lido and Sara. The baby was busy nursing at her mother's teat. Dave put his arm around me. Watching mom and foal, I wondered if younger mares tended to throw fillies. And if, as they got older, like Lusi, it was more common to see colts. *Miracles either way.*

The sun was high as noon approached, and Dave and I took leave of the reunion before heading to work. "But feel free to stay," I said to the group, "and enjoy the farm and the horses." As the centre of attention, Lusi, I was sure, would receive more than her fair share of peanut butter treats.

"By the way," the reporter said, "the article's going to appear in this week's Sunday edition, so watch for it."

On Saturday night a surprise showed up via email—the Sunday edition of the *Toronto Star* article and a video.

Tall and imposing, Dave stood with his blue eyes fixed on the camera. He came across as sincere and committed, and his chest puffed up each time he mentioned Illusionist's name. That night, we read and reread the article and watched the video until it was finally bedtime.

I got into bed and turned out my bedside light. "I'm wondering what page," I said.

Dave adjusted the papers on his nightstand. "Page?"

"You know, in the newspaper."

"We'll soon find out," he said, and turned off his bedside lamp.

Early on Sunday morning, I left Dave curled up in bed, threw on tattered, mismatched track clothes, and drove to the local grocery store. Too excited to fuss over myself, I glanced in the rear-view mirror and laughed. Framing my makeup-less face, curls stuck out sideways despite my finger-combing efforts en route.

At the store, I ran to the newspaper and magazine section and located the bold blue heading of the *Sunday Star*. A woman of Asian descent hovered above the pile of papers, already rummaging through the stack.

The horse image immediately caught my eye, so I assumed the woman had jostled the sections out of order. With a sigh, I took a step back. Something didn't make sense. The horse images seemed to be on the front page of each paper. How, at such an early hour, was it possible to mix up every single copy?

In my early morning stupor, it finally dawned on me. My head shot back and my knees buckled slightly. Lusi and Albert's story was front-page news. In the *Sunday Star*, no less—a publication with 300,000 subscribers all through the greater Toronto area and nearby cities, towns, and municipalities.

Regaining my balance, I dived for a copy. The bolded crimson headline read, "HAPPY ENDING TO

A HEARTBREAKING DILEMMA." I froze on the lino-leum tile.

In the accompanying photo, Darlene, Derrick, Lusi, and Albert stood proud and healthy with the country beauty of Hillsborough Stables in the background. The "once in a lifetime" significance hit me. I bent and snatched a handful of copies.

The woman watched my frenzied grab from less than a foot away. Standing so close, I tucked in my chin and closed my mouth, worried that she could smell my breath. Her mouth hung open and I was relieved I couldn't smell hers.

"Did you see the horses on the front page?" I said, waving a sample in the air with a crazy, wide grin on my face.

The woman nodded.

"It's the Year of the Horse," I said, happy to show off my knowledge of the Chinese calendar. "The article is about our horses."

The woman looked down at the copy in her hand, and then she looked up at me. Although I'd been present for the interview and my name was mentioned in print, my photo was conspicuously absent from the piece. The woman couldn't make a connection. I chuckled to myself as I jumped in the car and drove home. Playing a minor role in the written piece was somehow fitting, as none of the story would have happened had it been up to me.

All day long, emails and text messages poured in from friends and family. Dr. Arroyo was excited about the nod in the article to all the good vet medicine. I texted a response to him that read,

Quick, somebody call Disney.

I added some smiling emojis for effect.

My good friend Kelly, who lived in Toronto and knew of Lusi and Albert's dilemma, sent a text that read,

Really? The front page!

Nobody could believe it. Here in the Standardbred racing world, where men and women worked hard for the creatures they loved and respected, front-page publicity from *the Star* was not a common occurrence. Emails showered the folks at Hillsborough Stables and the veterinary centre in Guelph. Encouraging messages from strangers, both within Canada and beyond North America, praised everyone's efforts, love, and devotion.

Dave walked around beaming. He'd never wavered; he'd known all along that saving Albert was the right thing to do.

"More cards and emails today," I said, standing at the kitchen island. The rustling of papers filled the air. "This one's from Costa Rica."

"You sound surprised." He read the messages over my shoulder and skimmed the envelopes.

"You know," I said, "I still feel as if I don't deserve all this kindness from people we've never even met. *You* deserve it, but not me. Because I saw Albert as a lost cause. And yet unlike Lusi, who's aloof with me, he gives me kisses."

Dave smiled. "Lusi is Lusi. Albert loves you."

"Albert loves everyone, including me," I said. I felt a lump growing in my throat. Knowing how hard I fought to build a case to end the preemie's life would always haunt me. I wondered if over time, Albert, with his gentle, responsive ways, would help heal my self-inflicted wounds and allow me to forgive myself.

But I couldn't wonder about that for long, because just over a week after the newspaper article appeared, and not long after Lido's red bag delivery, a concerned Darlene called Dave about baby Sara.

Chapter 5

TWELVE DAYS

I overheard Dave curse softly under his breath. Sara was having problems. Everyone agreed that the little filly needed a level of care beyond simply a veterinary house call.

Dave entered the kitchen. "Sara's been admitted to the hospital in Guelph."

"Lido too?" I asked. "She's nursing."

Dave leaned heavily against the table with both hands. "They're together."

"I can't figure it out. We just saw Sara and she looked like a normal, happy foal," I said, as I snaked my way between the sink, fridge, and island, anxiously wiping the counters and fussing for no reason.

"This happens sometimes. Darlene said so," Dave said. He took his glass of water into the family room and plopped down on the couch.

"The vet hospital will take care of things. After all, they did a great job saving Lusi and Albert." Standing in the empty kitchen, I felt as if I were giving myself a pep talk.

With the day's trash bag in hand, I took a good look at Dave on my way to the garage. His eyes were glued to some imaginary nowhere space in front of him. He sat with one fist clenched and didn't even reach for the TV converter.

"I guess there's always the risk of infection in a placenta-first situation," I shouted from the mud room. "But it sounded like the delivery went so well otherwise." I came in and sat beside Dave. "I know she's not even a week old, but the baby seemed so healthy when we saw her." I laced my fingers in Dave's, sensing his level of worry was moving from a simmer to a boil. It certainly was for me.

Buzz. Buzz. Dave's cell phone vibrated across the coffee table. He squinted at the message. "It's pneumonia, Renata. They've started Sara on IV antibiotics."

I resisted the urge to make the sign of the cross. "Let's hope and pray that works."

When she arrived in Guelph, Sara was still nursing, active, and alert. After the first twenty-four hours of care, the vet in charge called Dave and said, "There's been some improvement in breathing, and things are less laboured."

Dave and I reassured each other that mare and foal would soon be back at Hillsborough Stables. After going through so much health drama with Lusi and Albert just over two months earlier, a little pneumonia was easy for the vets—or so we told ourselves before we headed back up to Guelph the next day.

Stalled together, Lido and Sara seemed locked in some sort of silent conversation. The intuitive new mother had a unique intelligence, I thought. Observing from the shedrow, I felt that Lido sensed her baby was struggling. Although Sara did initially perk up and show improvement, she began to deteriorate a few days later.

On April 19, nearly a week after being admitted to the veterinary hospital, Sara died.

The veterinary team, in consultation with Dave and Darlene, chose to leave the foal's body in the stall. Lido nudged and sniffed her lifeless filly, all the while uttering the softest of nickering sounds. In her own way, she seemed to be trying to awaken her newborn baby from its permanent slumber. Although unable to communicate with her caregivers or us, it was evident from Lido's sad eyes and listless manner that she knew Sara would not be coming to life again.

Trudging from the animal hospital to our car that day was a low point for us, and for our little herd.

"I can't believe it," I muttered through a Kleenex-covered nose and mouth. My tears soon saturated the few tissues I could find in my coat pockets.

"Pneumonia is tough, Renata," Dave said, his face flushed and his eyes red.

"I know. But twelve days old. I just thought that after Albert, we'd have some better luck with Sara." I closed the car door. Sitting in the idling car, I sobbed. We both sobbed and held each other, until at last Dave put the car into drive and headed toward the highway.

I closed my eyes. The car engine hummed within the otherwise quiet vehicle. My clearest memory of sweet Sara with the bright white star hung in front of me. Without opening my phone to review photos, I could see Lido licking and cleaning her baby—the little one's eyes on the camera as if to show off her newness and beauty. Poor darling filly, I thought. Dave pressed a napkin into my hand.

There was irony intertwined with our grief. In the past, we'd been notoriously late at naming newborn foals. We always felt pressure to come up with a gracious and unique name befitting of the bloodlines, which took time. In this instance, we immediately picked Sarasota Magic. During the precious foal's short life and subsequent demise, Dave and I were glad to have named her and given Sara the respect and dignity she deserved.

In the late afternoon that same day, we got word from Guelph. Lido hadn't eaten her dinner. The veterinarians told Dave that, instead, she had stood silent with her head hung low beside Sara.

We arranged to donate the foal's remains to the veterinary school, and not long after sunset, Lido went home to Hillsborough Stables without her baby. The mare had been given a mild sedative for the short trip, and she loaded onto the trailer like a ghost of her former self. From the time Darlene and Derrick unloaded the trailer, they made every effort to make Lido comfortable with a clean stall and her favourite food. They promised to stay close by and be there to offer her an extra smile or a loving rub.

That first evening, they told us they could hear Lido calling out for her baby. The sounds gradually became less desperate.

Back home in Ancaster, Dave and I comforted each other. It was late. Reading Darlene's texts over Dave's shoulder made my heart sink for Lido's loss. "How long?" I said, nearly choking on my words.

Dave reached over and rubbed my back. "How long what?"

"Do horses mourn?" I said. I looked down, because I knew if I looked at him that I'd start sobbing again, and I might not be able to stop.

"It's hard to say," Dave murmured through his sniffles.

"Losing a child is unimaginable." I swallowed hard. The unspoken rose up between us, hovering like a shadow. Dave and I had both wanted children, but fate had decided it was not to be. I reached into the box of tissues and grabbed a handful. "So sad."

Dave nodded and turned out the kitchen light.

Arm in arm, we headed up the stairs to bed.

The darkness brought order to my thoughts and feelings: Hillsborough Stables, with big open wooden doors, contained charitable, loving hearts that cared for and reached out to all the horses in the barn, including ours. A Hillsborough Stables that pulsed with life was always noisy, and that noise had a name: it was happiness. That comforting place—where more than a dozen pointy-eared heads would peek out at us, each a beacon of light in our darkened equine world—was where we knew we'd eventually go to work through our grief and confusion.

Dave and I went back to work the next day. On the outside, we carried on as if all was fine and normal in our lives. It wasn't something you could bring up out of the blue with friends or co-workers, but at least we had each other during an otherwise difficult time.

For days, weeks, and months, we visited Lido and watched as she endured. Everyone connected to the horse and Hillsborough did his or her best to visit our four-year-old more often. Lido's udder went back to normal. Gradually, her body reconfigured itself back to its longer, less round pre-pregnancy Standardbred state. She seemed to brush her brief period of motherhood into the past.

Derrick and Darlene made extra trips down the mare's shedrow and traded observations and updates with each other and us. They didn't rush the horse to socialize, or to get back to a routine. Eventually, Lido was paddocked with a maiden horse. The new friendship with the young chestnut mare who'd never been pregnant seemed to help. Dave and I often trekked along the picturesque path behind the barn to visit Lido over the course of her recovery. The wind blew in her mane and in our faces, and we hung out along the fence line for long stretches of time. Through loving words, attention, and delicious offerings, Dave and I tried to comfort Lido as best we knew how.

On the drives back home, I always took the time to pause and think. The sunbeams reflecting through the passenger window warmed my skin, and the odd slow-down due to a meandering tractor, with mud flying off its back wheels, had a strange, soothing effect on me. I understood that all the successes, like Albert's and Lusi's survival earlier in the year, were simply counterweights to Sara's death and Lido's dissipating grief. In the vast farmer's field of life, where good and bad alternated, I convinced myself, and Dave, that the positive would soon arrive and replace the negative in Lido's case. Along the route that spring of 2014, we assured each other that Lido's time to be a mother would come again soon enough.

We were wrong about Lido's time. And we were more than surprised by the unexpected direction our equine-related decisions would take us this late in our lives. One of those directions was going to bring about the biggest purchase we would ever make. It would stretch Dave's generosity and patience and test our relationship to each other and to our small herd.

But first, another new direction beckoned me, and took me down a creative path I'd never before dreamed possible—or even considered.

Chapter 6

SWITCHING GEARS

More than a month had passed since the *Sunday Star* article and Sara's death. I was wandering through the house with a basket of clothes in my arms when I stopped mid-hallway and stood staring at Dave. He was watching sports and sifting through a pile of mail, one cat on his lap and another sprawled on the floor beside him. The low hum of the TV allowed me to focus my thoughts before I spoke.

"Don't you see?" The level of emotion in my voice surprised me.

"See what?" Dave sat up, jolted to attention.

"Albert and Lusi's story spoke to people."

"Yeah?" Dave eyed me.

"Imagine if they knew everything?" I said. "About Albert, Lusi, Lido, Sara, all the horses and us." The basket shifted in my hands and I nearly spilled the socks folded on top.

"You'd need more than a front-page article to cover that one," Dave said, with a chuckle.

"Don't laugh." I stood up straighter, as if appearing taller might underscore the tone of my words.

"What?" Dave brought down the volume on the TV.

"I've made a decision," I announced. A few quiet seconds hung in the air.

"Yes?" Dave finally said, his eyes gleaming with curiosity.

"I'm going to tell the story of Lusi, Albert, and our little herd," I blurted. "I'm going to write a book!"

"Good," Dave shot back.

His reaction surprised me. "I mean it."

"Me too," Dave said.

Joy and Martha were both looking up at me. Joy was lying face forward on Dave's lap with her two front paws tucked under her body, while Martha now sat upright on the hardwood floor in front of me. Even the cats seemed to be interested in my announcement.

"You think I can?" I said.

Dave gathered a handful of empty envelopes in one hand and pointed them in my direction. "You're steadfast and persistent." His eyes locked on mine. "I couldn't do it—but you could."

"Well. You know I'm mad about everything paper." I smiled. "And I can type about eighty words per minute." Joy chose that moment to give a long, dismissive-sounding meow. I laughed out loud. "It's a great story, but what if I write something terrible?"

"At least it'll be a start." Dave gave Joy a few quick strokes on the head. "Then you can make it better over time."

Standing there grasping the basket and thinking about the writing task, I was momentarily filled with doubt and anxiety. As a person who'd never written a book and didn't even like English class in high school, what was I thinking? I took a deep breath, and the air helped me regain my focus and enthusiasm.

"Can I bounce things off you?"

"Of course!" Dave said. "And I'll help keep the racing facts straight too."

Dave didn't know anything about writing books, but he was the right person to co-commit to this project. He had a keen mind for seeing possibilities and alternatives. He knew our horses, their stories, and the world of harness racing better than anyone else I knew.

That night in bed, with all the peace and quiet in the house, I had plenty of time to think, and what I thought about was writing a book. Despite the business of my career, working full time forever—no maternity leave or time off—first as an X-ray technologist and then teaching X-ray technology, I'd been telling Dave for more than a decade that I wanted to write a book. It was just one of those things I repeated, such as "I should dye my hair lighter to better hide the grey." He wasn't surprised.

I'd kept a journal since grade school. I'd also started two books in the past and never got around to finishing either one. My inclination to write in a serious way began before I'd finished my master's degree in medical education. The real secret was that I already thought of myself as a writer of sorts. I'd written tons of memos, emails, and course manuals throughout my career as both an administrator and a technologist in the X-ray field, and then in teaching, as a professor and program coordinator.

A decade plus was a long time to carry around the desire to write something big and meaningful. All these years I'd felt expectant, but not in the traditional "pregnant" sense: I was swollen with at least two books—fraternal twins—floating around inside me. This time was going to be different. The horses—Lusi, Albert, Magic, Lido, Sara—were inspiring me to give the book idea another try.

The next morning I woke, and without thinking or even washing, I sat down at my desk and began writing. I had almost no idea what I was doing, but I figured I might as well get started.

At the heart of it all, I wanted to make up for the recent and distant past: for the harm I'd caused, or almost caused, because of my long-time, strong-willed insistence on science above all else; and for my resulting sin of believing Albert should be euthanized and the collateral pain this must have caused Dave, who believed otherwise.

The book's trajectory covered our lives from 2001 to 2014. Sifting through old memories at the racetrack and training barn allowed thoughts and emotions from our younger married days to bubble up to the surface. The vivid reflection required to tell a true horse story shocked and scared me at times. Alone, laughing hysterically one minute and literally crying the next during each tip-tapping session, I saw the word count expand.

Writing about Lusi, her pregnancy, and motherhood, my mind caught an old memory and shifted without warning. I recalled a period decades earlier, after a difficult significant event in our lives. This would be Lusi's last pregnancy, though she didn't know it. In my case, I had known it all too well.

At twenty-seven and married to Dave for three years, I expected my life to be relatively mainstream and traditional. My parents had mapped it all out, or at least planted the seeds in my mind. Someday I'd have boyfriends, then a husband, children, and a career—in that order. All our friends had started having babies.

After a miscarriage, I convinced myself and Dave that the fertility-clinic route was the next logical step. Given we were both young, healthy adults, the odds were in our favour. I took the pills the doctor offered and bingo! It happened. We got pregnant on the first cycle. By the seven-week mark, however, things took an unexpected turn. I was already experiencing vomiting—a normal symptom of pregnancy—but cramping and severe neck pain signalled something more ominous.

The sun was hot on that August long weekend in 1991. I awoke, still groggy from surgery. The physician's words sounded like they were meant for someone else. *Was she talking about me?*

"It was an ectopic—tubal—pregnancy," she was saying. "There was a lot of internal bleeding—close call for a transfusion. The right tube was removed." She put a hand on my shoulder. "You'll make a full recovery. You'll be fine."

When I'd recovered, Dave and I redoubled our baby-making efforts. However, despite decades of unprotected intimacy, I never did get pregnant. Instead of looking into other options, Dave and I counted our blessings in other regards and came to terms with being a child-free couple.

Over time, I realized, my love for the horses had started to fill a void I'd forgotten long ago. My sorrow from the deep distant past, preserved perfectly intact, was now suddenly exposed to light and air. I couldn't stop myself from feeling again the way I had in my twenties, helpless and horrified. But now the writing gave me strength.

I jumped into the task hooves first, starting with Albert's and Lusi's medical records. Each horse's file rivalled the weight and thickness of a volume of the *Encyclopaedia Britannica*. I sifted through the veterinary charting and reports for hours at a time, thankful for my background in X-ray and my knowledge of medical terminology. Dave helped me fill in any veterinary holes I couldn't seem to recall.

A stack of paperbacks also littered the floor beside me, each one a variation on the same theme—writing. Apart from *The Green Mile*, I'd never cared too much for Stephen King's printed works. However, his book *On Writing* was another story. I gobbled the pages—then reread it.

The important people in my life—Dave, my parents, and my sisters—were behind me. Mom supplied the title, *The Bounty of Illusionist*, although she advised me to wait and see if Albert would make it to the racetrack. In my mind, the story was too unusual and too happy to wait another minute. So I soldiered on. The writing process encouraged me to expand as a person and reach for something beyond my old self. I wanted people to see, through my writing, the positive side of the Standardbred racing world. And for the sake of all the equine individuals involved, I wanted to highlight their intrinsic value, not as disposable commodities but as living beings—those hardworking four-legged athletes with personality, majesty, and heart. But was that enough?

I'd read that most writers eased into the craft with short stories and articles by the dozens. Day after day, I worked only on *The Bounty of Illusionist*. I read a lot and wrote a lot. I felt my skills were improving and I grew more optimistic about my storytelling ability. I was certain the book would get published, and so was Dave.

Well... The first draft was beyond bad. It unexpectedly morphed into chapters filled with details about the strong bond between two committed people during life's unexpected ups and downs. Somehow, Lusi ended up hovering like a movie extra in between the mid-ground and the background, and so did Albert, the other horses, and harness racing.

The lousy initial version of *The Bounty of Illusionist* came to life through an online short-story course. The content and curriculum of the course exposed me—a science-minded individual—to items I'd run from in the past. My previous education was kind of lopsided. I liked math, chemistry, and physics. For every decent grade I earned in subjects requiring mathematics, I got 70s in English and even lower grades in languages during high school.

Now the topics and corresponding readings were wrapped up in a handful of small online writing assignments. I was learning serious stuff such as plot, characterization, point of view, setting, and narrative. Oh God, then there was the dreaded grammar! It was like an old classmate I'd consciously abandoned as early as middle school. The educational *Schoolhouse Rock* songs of my youth often played inside my head. I'd sometimes catch myself humming the tunes.

The course involved two major assignments. One consisted of a first draft of the narrative, and the final assignment involved turning that draft into a longer, polished piece. The first draft allowed me to open the horse-story floodgates.

Night after night, I stared with a mixture of delight and disbelief at the electronic mass of words before me. The page count for the first draft had already topped out at twenty-eight. Describing Hillsborough Stables, the horses, the people, and the barn birds in flight, I could sit and write setting all day long. I knew I was in trouble: the story moved forward at a perceptibly slow pace and there wasn't a single stitch of dialogue. I was too afraid to use quotation marks. By the time late spring rolled around, though, I'd mapped out the entire narrative arc for *The Bounty of Illusionist*.

"I saw the horses today," Dave said. He started to set the table.

"How's Lusi?" I said. "Is Albert still chewing her tail?" The timer went off.

"Her tail *is* pretty short now. Albert chews the belly bandage too." He shook his head and helped me strain the pot of boiled squash. "By the way, Darlene, Derrick, and I talked a bit about farm real estate today."

"Do they seem optimistic?" I said.

"Yes." Dave finished setting the table. "We're focusing on location."

"That's key, right?"

Dave nodded. "So—how goes the writing course?"

I bit my lip, not entirely appreciating the sudden shift in topic. "Huh? I guess it's okay."

"Must be nearly finished."

I took a long breath. "Well…" I started and stammered, then managed to say it. "I'm not handing in the final assignment." I set the piping hot plates of food on the table and sat down.

"Really." Dave shot me a quizzical look. He applied the corkscrew to a wine bottle and started twisting.

Feeling the need to confess, yet wanting him to know I'd somehow succeeded, I said, "I already passed the course."

The wine bottle opened with a slight pop. "What's the issue?" Dave said.

"I don't merely want a short story about our horses. I want a whole book." I fiddled with my cutlery. "I've got my eye on a creative writing course at the local college that starts soon. And there's also a writing conference coming up."

Dave smiled. "Sounds good."

"The book about Lusi, Albert, and us has officially started." I raised my wine glass. "Cheers."

I hadn't taken a face-to-face class in decades unless you counted tai chi, cooking, and making twig chairs. More than twenty years after finishing my diploma in radiography and my bachelor's degree in biology, I'd completed my master's in medical education via distance learning. So, when the next step in the book-writing process seemed to guide me toward a creative writing class, my stomach had lurched forward, nearly showing me the day's menu at the prospect of being part of a group. But I signed up anyway.

Once a week for a few hours, I and a dozen other students—mainly female—worked alone and in teams, writing and refining, under the guidance of our instructor. The in-person learning environment didn't produce a completed book as I'd expected, but it felt right. When I started, I only had a hammer and all I saw were nails. Thanks to the course, my writing toolkit evolved.

During that time, the horses were doing well. Unlike us, they were unaware of the turmoil surrounding harness racing in Ontario. They had no idea they'd need a new home in a few months, when the expensive Hillsborough lease ended. To help Derrick and Darlene, Dave had started checking the internet for farms for rent. Sometimes we talked about other possible Lumsden-family arrangements to lessen the financial outpouring, such as selling Lido. It was all talk, because it never went anywhere. We were just two people trying to do the best we could for our horses and ourselves, and our commitment to our herd had expanded now to encompass pages in a book.

After the creative writing course, I still felt the need for support, specifically in the form of one-on-one guidance. So I ventured out to the Ontario Writers' Conference in Ajax, Ontario.

The sun radiated golden beams and white clouds dotted the sky as I drove across Toronto in the early morning hours. Nestled beside me on the front seat was a bulging envelope. Its contents included a first draft of the completed manuscript, a one-minute story synopsis, and a rough draft of a query letter—to be sent to literary agents and publishers in the hopes of interesting them in my book. All the way there I repeated the synopsis, hoping it would sink into my memory before I reached my destination. For a small extra fee, I'd secured a session with an agent.

My time had come, I thought, when the literary agent would smile. I sat down. The first ten pages of my manuscript took up 90 percent of the tiny wooden table space between us. Watching the agent read through my materials, I panicked. *Just listen*, I told myself, which calmed my nervous excitement. At last she spoke.

"Always ask, where is Lusi in all of this?" she said. "It's about the horse."

The agent's words enlightened me. Motivated to focus on the mare I loved, I drove home. In a month's time, I'd rewritten the entire manuscript.

I now had a second first draft, or technically, a terrible second draft. But the book and the horses' stories became an obsession. Writing a book contained all the elements of creation. It wasn't a baby, but it began as a speck and then, with nurturing, it formed over days, weeks, and months. Eventually, after a year and a half, an undeniable truth hit me. A new thing had emerged, something I'd created that hadn't existed before. I stared at the computer and ran the cursor up and down the side margin. I'd written Lusi and Albert's story. *The Bounty of Illusionist* was going to happen. And, like the horses, it was going to take me on a whole new journey.

Chapter 7

UNEXPECTED TWISTS AND TURNS

Historically, foaling season could easily be described as a roller coaster ride for owners, midwives, and horses. Predicting due dates of pregnant mares was as tricky as timing the delivery of human babies, but estimates were often correct within a week or two. When mid-January rolled around, the slow, steady climb started as the birth of the first foal loomed. Resident mares with bulging bellies began to wax, and so did pregnant mares that had been shipped over to Hillsborough Stables just for the happy occasion. And all of a sudden, whipping down from that enormously high peak, the first foal arrived. Then week after week, mare after mare, more and more foals were born over the next several months. Pure and beautiful, each new life held the promise of the next rising star within the sport. Darlene and Derrick's sleep–wake patterns and eating habits were turned upside down. They morphed into vampire-like characters and seemed to enjoy the familiar, yet deranged, ride.

The foaling season of 2014 was different. Calm hovered over the barn and within the stalls. The usual pulse and pressure was more intermittent. The lull-time between births allowed other farm-related work to continue. We had expected two foals—one from Lusi and the other from Lido. Fifteen foals in total were due at the farm—a steep drop compared with the past that normally saw the Hillsborough Stables roller coaster deliver thirty to forty bright new faces into Derrick's and Darlene's capable hands.

While nobody ran around pointing fingers at the reason or culprit behind the change, this decline was, of course, the result of those Ontario government cutbacks to the horse-racing industry in 2012. The cancellation of SARP caused a violent earthquake in the Ontario racing industry, and the aftershocks continued to play out two years later, bringing change and stress to all those involved and turning up the volume on unpredictability for horses and the people around them.

Our small herd was not excluded from the casualties when Dave and I were forced to make some tough horse-related decisions. Reluctantly, we sold some of our best horses, taking our stable numbers from a high point of five actively racing down to one—keeping Lusi's second daughter, Mach Magic. And then there were some horse-related surprises later in 2014 we didn't see coming.

"I got a call from Ridgewood Farm," Dave announced as he dropped the grocery bags on the kitchen island with his keys and wallet.

I spotted the eggs and started unpacking. "Ridgewood? What about?"

"Pan and Shorty." Dave's face was calm but his fists were clenched.

An image of our two sweet-faced geldings, both retired racers, came into my mind. "Everything okay with them?" The sentence seemed to take all my breath away.

Dave picked up the cereal boxes and pushed them into the pantry. "The horses can't stay there anymore."

My hands flew up to my face in surprise and I dropped a container of yogourt. "But why?"

"It's tough out there, Renata," Dave said.

I started fussing over the wet white mess on the counter. "They need to leave? How long do they have?"

"They need to leave soon."

Dave explained the situation. The two women who had taken in our geldings years earlier also did some Standardbred training, and racing. But they had felt the effects of the government's reversal and could no longer stay focused on harness racing. Their farm sale happened quickly, and the closing date was fast approaching. They'd rented a small house and property with no room for horses. Their new plans included lessening daily expenses such as horse feed, vaccinations, worming, vet work, and farrier costs, in an effort to rebuild their dwindling finances.

"Winter's coming." I rubbed the back of my neck. Winter meant no grass for grazing. It meant paying for hay. Sometimes it meant investing in blankets. Winter was an expensive time to find homes for horses.

"I know," Dave said. His eyes were soft and his expression understanding.

We sat contemplating the turn of events. I ran my fingers through my hair, stopping to massage my temples now and then while my thoughts came into focus. I exhaled loudly while Dave's face remained calm.

At fifteen years old, Pan and Shorty had limited options. Selling them at auction might fetch a small price, if they sold at all. And then where might they end up? The image of both horses pulling a buggy day after day came to my mind. Whether mythological or real, the after-racing life of a buggy horse was talked about within the Standardbred industry. Some buggy drivers supposedly worked the horses from dusk to dawn, until the horses dropped. Then, as now, few horse lovers were looking for a pasture ornament or companion horse, and the idea of the two boys ending up at slaughter made me feel nauseous.

"Those hardworking old horses need a home," I said. We owed them that. After all, Pan had been our first.

It was some kind of unpredictable good luck that took Dave and me, for that matter down the horse ownership trail some ten years earlier in 2004.

Are You Pan Enough was a handsome red bay gelding. A spark ran through me when we were introduced. I kept my distance and stared.

With a massively muscular neck, Pan, as we called him, stood about 15 hands high.[5] Dave thought nothing of the horse's smaller-than-average size. My husband could tell, even from the distant public grandstands at Toronto's Woodbine racetrack, where he claimed[6] five-year-old Pan: the horse had the athletic prowess to compete at a high level.

Pan was our king of the half-mile tracks, which allowed spectators and owners like us a closer look at the racing action thanks to the smaller circumference. Dave and I staggered with giddy enthusiasm around the winner's circle on many occasions with Pan. The horse won nearly fifty races in his career. Dave called Pan "Pan the Man." The horse was a friend to us.

From time to time, Are You Pan Enough showed signs of lameness, especially during the sticky, hot summer months.

---

5   A "hand" equals four inches; horses are measured from the ground to their withers, where the neck joins the body.

6   In a claiming race, the horses in the race are all for sale for more or less the same price.

Each and every time, the investigation revealed the same problem—an abscess. It was the horse's one physical weakness. Sometimes an errant pebble from the track or a puncture from a sharp object caused the horse to limp. Either scenario ended up creating a pus pocket. Consistent foot care was the key to keeping the horse sound.

When Pan would come up lame, the trainer, groom, or vet would discover a "hot spot," or abscess, and drain it. Once cleaned out, the affected hoof was soaked in a simple home remedy. After each and every race competition, just to be on the safe side, all four feet got the same treatment—Epsom salts and warm water. The only way the trainer could keep Pan interested and quiet enough to stand with each leg in its own bucket was to slowly feed the gelding his favourite treat. Pan was our first peanut-butter granola bar addict. He started it all.

At the Victory Lane training facility in Freelton, Ontario, Pan occupied the stall near the entrance. From there, he could see and hear Illusionist, the spirited new mare, directly across the shedrow kicking the walls. With eyes in a sinister pinch, she often shot Pan a wild, shrill neigh. The two racehorses, Lusi and Pan, were stall-mates from 2004 to 2009, when Lusi retired. Pan hung up his harness-racing hobbles[7] twelve months later, in 2010.

Where handsome Pan, the rich red bay, was intelligent, with an athletic superiority that required more than a modicum of respect, Shorty Bones was a less showy brown bay with an easygoing manner. The pair of gifted racehorses could not have been more different in personality. Pan was self-aware and acted entitled, like royalty; Shorty was curious and friendly—enough to warrant careful supervision. If

---

7   Equipment used to maintain the horse's gait. The leather straps connect the front and rear legs on the same side.

curiosity killed the cat, then Shorty's mischievous horse antics during downtime between racing and training drove nearby grooms and trainers to keep favoured belongings— food, clothing, fingers and toes—far from the horse's reach. Shorty shredded everything within grabbing distance: toys, tools, shoes, lunch bags, and winter coats included.

Any horseman coming through the training barn would have noticed Shorty second. However, the two horses had something special in common. Both performed their best on the racetrack with Dave behind them as owner. With Shorty especially, there was a real empathy between horse and human.

Like Pan, Shorty also came to Dave as a five-year-old. The condition of both horses wasn't a joke back then, but we could laugh about it now. Pan came into our lives with bad feet, and Shorty with a bad leg. Athletic horses got athletic injuries. Shorty had what horsemen referred to as a bowed tendon, but Dave didn't know it when he claimed the horse. Massive muscles initially hid the horse's subtle defect. Damaged tendon fibres from repeated high-level competition resulted in a "bowed" appearance to the leg upon healing. With torn tendons in one leg, Shorty was more likely to have trouble staying sound.

The Standardbred breed has always competed—as pacers or trotters—and is now primarily bred for competition. An individual racehorse's desire to compete, however, is something that comes naturally from within. Intuitively, we sensed that racing for Shorty was more than an act of athletic stamina; it was an act of joy. Shorty wanted to race and please us, and we wanted to let him do it.

On competition days, instead of catching snippets of restful and restorative sleep, Shorty flared his nostrils and plumed his tail in excitement. In his career, Shorty had eighty-two racing starts and "made the podium" forty-eight times. As far as the bowed tendon went, we managed it as best we could, all the while keeping an eye on the horse's well-being. With a will to win at all costs, Shorty raced on the big oval from 2002 to 2006, his final two years with Dave as owner.

Being sentimental as well as a responsible owner, Dave wanted to control where Shorty landed at the end of his career. In early 2007, my husband canvassed everyone he knew in the industry until he found a suitable place, and the gelding retired into the welcoming hands of the two women at Ridgewood Farm. That year, they sent Christmas cards featuring Shorty romping in the snowy paddock. To our relief and delight, when Pan retired nearly four years later, the same women offered him a spot to join his pal Shorty and enjoy a well-earned retirement.

But now our two geldings were about to become homeless.

"It'll work out." Dave grabbed my hand and squeezed.

"What if Derrick and Darlene don't find a farm?" I said. "What will happen to Pan, Shorty, and the rest of our horses and theirs?"

"Don't worry," he said. "Pan and Shorty won't end up in a slaughter pen."

Dave got busy the following day. He made some calls, and Darlene and Derrick agreed to take the pair of horses. They were familiar with the boys from their racing days; Shorty Bones and Are You Pan Enough had both spent time at Hillsborough Stables.

At the same time that we gained, or rather regained, Pan and Shorty, we lost a very fast horse named Pontiac Luck. A strong, strapping gelded bay, Pontiac Luck headed south of the border to a new owner and trainer in the USA. Down in the States, the horse would continue to race at the same high level he raced for us but would make double in race-win earnings, due to the high purses at Yonkers in New York State.

We chose to let go of Pontiac, as we called him, but it was a hard decision. He was our friend and we were so proud of him. Twice the horse competed in PEI for us with Dave cheering in the grandstands at the historic Gold Cup & Saucer race. We hung our heads low when Pontiac pulled out of our herd. The sacrifice hurt. But amid all the uncertainty caused by the government, it was a safe decision for Pontiac and for our other horses, since the money the horse fetched couldn't go lame. Those funds could go toward caring for all the mouths we still had to feed.

On the spring day that the trailer came to fetch Pontiac, Dave and I decided to stay home. Seeing him leave would have been too painful.

"He's gone." I wiped the wet from both eyes with my hands. "So many have come and gone."

"The horses—remembering and talking about them is part of us," Dave said.

"Pontiac was good to us," I said.

"We'll never forget him or the others." Dave gave me a half grin with red, sunken eyes.

I jumped up from the kitchen table. Wrapping my arms around him, I pulled him close and we rocked back and forth. "And don't forget about Albert," I whispered.

We both laughed. But deep down we were worried. Dave was right. It was tough out there. Where would Albert, Lusi, and our little herd end up if Darlene and Derrick couldn't find something suitable to rent?

Chapter 8

BRINGING UP BABY

Magical Albert was, of course, oblivious to our concerns. He was focused on feeding and growing. From his arrival at Hillsborough Stables in February to late summer of 2014, Albert enjoyed his blue buckets of milky delight. Feedings occurred hourly for the first few months. Then they shifted down to every two hours, and then four hours, and then finally to four times per day or every six hours.

Familiarity with orphaned foals—sometimes through rejection by the mare or by an untimely negative event during birth—meant it was hardly the first time Darlene and Derrick had shared sleep-deprived feeding responsibilities. It left the couple in a zombie state for all of winter and spring, and into summer.

Albert loved the warm vanilla-flavoured concoction, and he also loved anyone carrying the navy-blue bucket that the milk replacer always came in. The horse was particularly close to his mother, Lusi, but he adored Derrick to pieces and may have thought Oscar was his very best four-legged buddy. Anytime Derrick entered Lusi and Albert's stall, the dog followed.

Since mother and son's happy reunion at the veterinary hospital, Lusi had always been hand-walked around her foal. She needed time to heal. Literally, for weeks. Albert trotted patiently beside his mom. Hand-walking Lusi with Albert alongside continued in the indoor arena at Hillsborough Stables as if it were normal behaviour for both. The youngster had never witnessed his mother burst forth. He'd never seen Lusi show off her true colours.

Usually, mares and their foals were socialized in small groups. Several mares and babies might share the same field. This way the young ones got to know each other while the mares stayed close for feeding and care. But Lusi and her son weren't socialized with other horses. They led contented lives together in their own paddock—that is, once they both made it to the spacious enclosure unattended.

The first day mother Lusi was allowed to run free, kicking her legs in the air out in the grassy paddock, her big, strong son took off running. Watching from a distance, Darlene and Derrick told us, they froze. Albert spotted them and headed in their direction. The midwives worried the youngster might jump the fence, or worse, get tied up in it. The barnboard laterals appeared to be enough to make Albert think otherwise, but the cardiac damage to the Hillsborough couple had occurred nonetheless.

"We've got to back things up," Darlene said, hands on her hips. "We can't have him running for the fences. Remember, Albert and Lusi were separated for ten days after his birth. He trusts humans more than his mother." She rubbed her chin.

"And Albert likes to do things his way," Dave said. "What do you think?"

I stood back listening as Darlene spelled out a plan.

"Back inside the arena they go," Darlene said. "Where the fences are higher—and stronger."

Dave thought for a moment and nodded. "It's safer for Albert."

"Lusi can run and buck," Darlene said. "Let Albert get used to her movements."

We all agreed the plan made sense.

Albert was like a rosebud, tightly wound; he took time to open. At first, he cantered around the enclosure with his mother, eventually running fast beside her. When Lusi kicked her back legs into the air, Albert kicked and twisted nearby. Our foal's fears regarding his mom's rapid bursts of joyful energy were abating. His progress into horse-hood was encouraging.

Eventually, many a short video clip sent from the farm showed our majestic boy outside prancing around in the warm breeze. Albert arched his back with a free and easy spirit about him, while Lusi grazed in the background. There was no rush to socialize the pair with other horses: one step at a time, Darlene thought, and Dave agreed.

Usually, foals had to be taught that humans represented a part of the good things in life. Albert was ahead on this lesson. In fact, he may have even thought *he* was human, because people, rather than his own mother, had given him warm cuddles during those first two weeks of his preemie life. For Albert, attention from humans had happened sooner and in a more concentrated fashion compared with most foals. He'd missed out on the usual first touch from a loving mother. Instead, each new shift at the animal hospital had brought another set of welcoming hands to love and care for him.

At Hillsborough Stables, Albert knew humans meant delicious surprises such as vanilla milk, peanut butter treats, carrots, and massages. The young horse enjoyed the tingly feeling of Derrick's hand as he lovingly scratched the foal's head and neck, and the pleasant, caring sound of a human voice. Our big bay boy would lean toward every loving pat, asking in the only way he knew that the attention never stop. Whenever Derrick, Dave, or I stroked Albert's forelock or mane, the youngster lowered his head and half closed his eyes, as if dreaming the most wonderful dream. Albert and Derrick were buddies, although Darlene frowned upon too much attention, saying, "It's not good for the foal." Darlene worried that Albert's desire to be close and to nuzzle would or could hurt someone as the horse grew. She may have been right. Albert accidentally stepped on my foot during one of our cuddles. Nothing fractured, but the skin tore open on three toes.

Big for his age, Albert stood out, especially compared with Angel.

Angel had been born five weeks premature to a Thoroughbred star of the racing circuit named Abbey. The mare had foaled out while Lusi and Albert were still in hospital. Scrawny and delicate, Angel weighed a mere fifty pounds at birth. Other than love and attention from Derrick, Darlene, and mother Abbey, the filly received no medical intervention and survived to thrive. Darlene told me that in her experience a natural birthing process, even if it occurred early, made a huge difference. Although Albert was only two weeks early, the midwife thought that the C-section delivery was far more traumatic, especially where the foal's lungs were concerned.

Week after week, month after month, all the foals at Hillsborough Stables filled out and matured. As a seven-month-old, Albert measured 14.3 hands, which made our beastie boy the tallest of them all and put him ever so much closer to his mom's height of 15.3 hands. And his weight, at six hundred pounds, definitely made him the biggest foal in the barn.

More noticeable, though, was Albert's personality. According to Derrick and Darlene, each morning when they entered the barn, Albert would lean his head against the stall bars. With one ear and one eye poking out, the colt tried to sneak a peek at the couple, and he always gave them a welcome good-morning nicker.

At morning turnout, if someone cleaned the waterers or cut through the paddock, Albert wandered from his mom to press up against their hands or nudge them with his nose. He begged for attention to some itch, real or imagined. He was nearly overbearing but never poorly behaved; he just revelled in his proximity to humans. We were told that all neonatal intensive-care foals behaved this way. We hoped that Albert's behaviour would turn out to be a positive legacy of his days under total human care, but only time would tell.

Then there was Albert's uncommon behaviour—the tongue sucking. He did that a lot around me. We heard Derrick say with a chuckle, "Never seen one do that before." Albert would press his tongue flat between his lips, letting the fleshy organ stick out sideways like a thin red worm. With his tongue out, the foal made sucking sounds after every treat—be it carrot or peanut butter bar. Albert seemed to be expressing a mix of affection, approval, and appreciation through the gesture. I thought the tongue sucking might be the horse equivalent of "Thanks so much for caring." Newcomers to the barn always stopped short when Albert showed off his thin red tongue.

Like all children, Albert tried his mother's patience. He was curious and became bored at albeit infrequent times, particularly when inside the stall. While Lusi still wore her C-section belly bandage, her son insisted on chewing and shredding the white cloth with his teeth. Derrick, Darlene, and the hired hands kept a watchful eye on the pair of horses.

Every day they trimmed and snipped the shredded bits of Lusi's bandage to prevent Albert eating them.

With the advent of warmer weather came the flies by day and mosquitoes by night. Mother and son huddled and slept in the safe confines of their spacious stall. Unfortunately for mother Lusi, Albert was a tail chewer. For the most part, tail chewing was common in foals, although annoying to the mare, whose tail was the target. Albert's tail-eating tendencies left Lusi little defence against bugs. She'd swat her tail at an insect and come up short. Albert chewed his mom's tail as some kids might suck on hair, and invariably ingested small quantities over time.

I tried a few remedies to deter the hair-eating monster, including tail "potion" and leave-in conditioner. The distasteful potion, similar to ones used on human thumb-suckers, and the hair conditioner simply left Lusi's tail a moist magnet for dirt. Neither liquid seemed to trouble Albert or dissuade him. Fortunately, our mare appeared to take it all in stride as part of the self-sacrifice of motherhood, and her eyes seemed to beam with pride at her son.

Despite his idiosyncrasies, Albert was considered a good boy at Hillsborough Stables. An energetic dervish of a foal, he was often busy defining himself against his world out in the paddock. High adventure seemed to await him in every butterfly, grasshopper, or gusty breeze that ruffled his coat. As the seasons changed, Lusi instilled in her foal all the life lessons possible, and Albert learned how to be a horse.

But even a neonatal intensive-care foal needed to grow up at some point. Weaning time—the time to separate mare and foal—had arrived. And with the nice weather and with winter sitting far away, it was also time to get serious about a new home for our friends at Hillsborough Stables.

Chapter 9

MOVING UP AND
MOVING ON

Derrick and Darlene had just returned from a trip to Ohio for the Little Brown Jug race—often considered the biggest Standardbred race for three-year-old pacing colts in North America.

"We gotta get the weaning done today," Darlene said to her husband.

Systematically, the couple proceeded stall by stall to separate the babies from their mothers. The foals had reached the five-month-old mark and all of them—filly or colt— were now skilled at eating grain and bulky food such as grass or hay. Weaning presented the opportunity for young horses to socialize with other horses their age and to learn new life skills within the herd environment. Darlene and Derrick knew that the older and bigger the young ones got, the more challenging they could be to handle during the process. They also knew the separation kept the babies safer: some mares were known to become exhausted and miserable. They might even start to resist nursing, a clear sign that they didn't want to deal with an annoying baby anymore.

We stood aside and watched.

They reached Lusi's stall. "I'll get Albert," Derrick said. He grabbed a halter and a short lead shank.

Albert backed away from Lusi. He lifted his head not toward the familiar stall, but to gaze out the door—toward his independence, perhaps? Eyeing his best human friend, Derrick, it was as if the youngster saw the future and the promise of great things to come—of happy times, new friends, races won, maybe even the siring of foals to carry on his mother's lineage.

Albert held still while Derrick slipped the halter on. Tightening his grip slightly, Derrick led Albert into the shedrow, leaving Lusi behind as the door closed. Our mare looked through the half-door opening. She let out a single whinny and went back to graze on her hay salad. Lusi knew. It was time.

Side by side, Derrick and Albert followed along the curved drive out back toward the main barn. Dave and I stayed a safe distance behind. The sun shone and birds swooped and chirped. Albert tossed his head a few times. He looked around with eyes wide. Then Albert and Derrick crossed the threshold and entered through the weathered double door.

Black rubber mats underfoot rolled out left and right along wide shedrows, which held accommodations for more than two dozen horses. The square stalls here with wooden sliding doors were smaller than the roomy double brood-mare stalls back at the foaling barn. The adjoining arena allowed all the inhabitants to gallop around and toss tails even in the icy-cold winter months. In the past, Albert had taken many laps there with his mother.

Derrick steered our foal away from the arena and around to the left. Albert's ears pricked. The horse stretched his neck as he eyed a number of young horses from his new vantage point. "Welcome to the weanling wing, Albert," Derrick said, as if to himself.

Born in January and now nearly eight months old, Albert was the oldest foal at Hillsborough. Babies born later in foaling season were at least five months old when weaning time rolled around. Foals weaned from their mothers were called weanlings until they reached their first birthday. On January first, all the young ones would be called yearlings.

To help with socialization efforts, Albert was stalled next to a fine chestnut with a distinctive, squiggly white blaze. Chester, his new neighbour, was closer to Albert's age and more importantly, his size.

Angel was stalled across the shedrow from the newly weaned boys. Her nose barely reached the opening between the stall bars. With attitude of her own, she squealed to announce her presence.

Over the next few months, Albert soaked up the sun and grazed during turnout time alongside a handful of weanling males.

In some herds, and with mares especially, establishing the pecking order was a rough business involving loud, teeth-baring confrontations. In Lusi's case, she was always near the top in dominance—some days at number one, and other days the odd bruise or bite meant she'd drifted down to number two or three. I never worried about Lusi. She could hold her own. Albert was a different story.

"I hope he's okay," I said, concerned that our preemie bottle-fed foal might be a shrinking violet and sink down the chain of command.

"Don't worry," Dave said. "Darlene and Derrick will keep an eye out."

In between chores, the midwife duo would wander over and stand behind a tree near the fence. They told us they saw

Albert at times push, nudge, and nip the others, a little bit like a bully.

I laughed when I heard about Albert's antics with his new friends. Dave did too. It made me wonder what type of bad human parents we would have been—Lido the prima donna, Lusi the wild matriarch, and Albert the bully. My goodness!

With weaning completed and the farm lease soon to expire, Dave, Darlene, and Derrick were ready to scout out the future in the form of a new, more affordable home for every horse, dog, and human at Hillsborough. Dave believed our horses were in the best hands. I agreed. He also believed that having our horses under one roof made the most sense. In his mind the most effective way to ensure the herd stayed together was to continue lending Derrick and Darlene a hand searching for their next location.

As it turned out, there was a lot more going on in Dave's mind, but it would take a little longer for me to find out exactly what he was thinking.

In life, Dave had always been focused on "the right thing to do." His sense of integrity was almost as sharp as his flip side of boundless common sense and calm, brainy focus. I knew that my husband, the businessman schooled in economics, had a talent for seeing alternatives other people might overlook. Helping Albert and Lusi was driving this momentum to find some solid ground in the present, but with the future of our herd in mind.

I was thrilled I'd met Dave in this life, because I suspected we might not see each other in the next. He would have saved Lusi over her unborn foal, I think, if it had come down to that, but his efforts—unlike mine—always involved both animals. Dave's focus on "the right thing to do" in Albert's case cost us a ton in vet bills. No evidence or argument from me back then, despite my utter certainty the foal would never see the outside of the veterinary hospital, could change his mind.

With self-preservation now hanging in the balance, Darlene, Derrick, and Dave took off. Driving along dirt, gravel, and paved roads, they visited potential properties from Flamborough through Ancaster to Campbellville. The list of "must haves" included a suitable home or living quarters, a specific barn space for both stalling and foaling horses, and a training arena. So many farm properties looked good on paper, but in reality were a disappointment.

"We found it," Dave said to me one afternoon. He dropped a real estate brochure on the table. Summer sunshine streamed in through the kitchen sliding door and bounced off the hardwood floor. "It's got an updated century-old house with four bedrooms and a finished basement. The property also has one barn that's in need of upgrading but is definitely worthwhile."

He grabbed a bottle of water from the fridge. "Oh," he said, "and I think we should buy it."

I stood there, a little stunned, and silent. The quiet allowed me to take in his words and process them.

In the distant past, Dave and I had discussed owning a farm. I should have known that one day it might happen. Clearly, for Dave the idea now of buying a farm instead of merely helping our friends find a place to rent sat right up there with the idea of saving a preemie foal. It sounded extreme, yet it niggled at me this time as "the right thing to do." Stability for our herd sat at the root of things.

"It's in Moffat, which is part of Milton, and its near Mohawk Raceway," Dave said. "That's an excellent bonus."

I agreed that it was. *The farm price? The opposite of excellent.* My finger traced the zeros.

"The herd can stay together, Renata," Dave said, "if we have a serious financial say in the location of their next home."

"I hear you."

Dave continued. "We'd add a second barn and training arena. The property's close to some large-animal vets too."

"Really?" I said. Dave looked at me and I'm sure my face showed a mix of confusion and interest. The idea of building barns and arenas stuck in my head. I had no idea about either.

"The farm's nearly one hundred acres, and it's got the right mix of land and nearly a dozen horse paddocks to start." He took a sip of water. "The house has geothermal and a well."

"Sounds like a contender." I felt a twinge of apprehension. "How much to build a barn?"

"Maybe seventy K, depending on the size and number of stalls." Dave tore into a new bag of chocolate chip cookies. "But I'm not really sure."

"The arena would be an added expense too? And you're not sure?"

"If we went ahead and built both at the same time," Dave said, "it could save us money."

Save money! I thought. "We don't even know what it will eventually cost, let alone how we'd pay for it." I shook my head. "Jesus! A seventy-K barn plus maybe an arena and then the cost of the property?" My mind did a backflip of calculations, flying through six figures and landing at seven.

"I think we should buy it," Dave said, with a straight face and cookies in his hand.

"I'm open to a new challenge, but farm owners might be a stretch, financially and otherwise, even for us." I picked up the agent's brochure.

It was unlike any I'd ever seen before. My finger bumped along the ring-bound spine. This wasn't a brochure; it was practically a book. The front cover read, "Welcome to Stonegate." I casually leafed through the pages. Printed on heavy matte paper, it held numerous colour images. They reminded me of magical places I'd read about as a child in so many classic fairy tales.

The main house at "Stonegate," though, was not exactly a little gingerbread house fit for Hansel and Gretel, but rather much sturdier and grander, with its chunky fieldstone exterior. While not on the scale of, say, Sleeping Beauty's castle, it might well suit a lord and lady of more modest means. And with its twenty-first-century upgrades, the place would definitely be witch-free, I thought.

"Where will we get the money?" I said, skimming over the pages. My eyes fixated on the rock-solid, fairy-tale wonder.

The house rested atop an elevated grassy area not far from the long barn below. A patchwork of paddocks outlined by worn wooden fences in a crosshatch design surrounded the structure. Towering beech, maple, and oak trees encircled the residence. Healthy in their canopy, they reached for the sky. Interspersed between the aged beech and oak tree monsters was an assortment of honeysuckle and lilac bushes. The circumference of their woody trunks spoke to the gardener in me; I could imagine the many decades of past bloom-growth and sleep cycles. In the distance it looked to me like the property trailed off to what must be enchanted woods. My heart pounded with the anticipation of next spring on this farm.

Standing at the kitchen island in Ancaster, I could almost feel the farm-fresh breeze and sunshine on my skin as I advanced through the colourful seller's brochure. Nowhere could I see any stone plaque or signpost. The name "Stonegate" appeared to be part of an advertising ploy by a smart real estate agent. (Once, we'd toured a house that was listed as "The Artist's Retreat.") "Stonegate" had a welcoming and solid ring to it. By the final page, I had silently convinced myself that buying the farm was the correct next step for Hillsborough Stables and us. How could any place so magical be a bad thing? After all, it was for Lusi, Albert, and all the horses living at Hillsborough Stables.

Dave hovered over my shoulder, taking in each page.

"You're right," Dave said, nodding. "We don't have that kind of money." He rubbed his chin and stared up at the ceiling. "We could sell the property by the lake."

My head jerked back in surprise.

Almost a decade ago, we'd bought a cottage on nearby Lake Erie, and then, with an eye to privacy, had purchased the rundown property next door to it as well. As custodian of the cottage, I found myself to be the most frequent visitor, keeping a close eye on things and monitoring all essentials like propane, water, and spider spraying. We thought the investment would awaken the latent cottage lover in us both. A place to soothe the soul and connect with nature, the cottage offered crystal-clear mornings fishing by a calm lake and dramatic red sunsets while enjoying chilled Chardonnay with a crackling bonfire dancing away in the backyard fire pit.

Or at least it was supposed to.

I shot Dave a look but stood quiet. Thinking.

"The math doesn't work," I said. "We'd still need a lot more."

"Then we'd borrow a chunk against our house," Dave said, quickly adding before I could speak, "Hillsborough Stables would be the tenant. They would look after maintenance and help pay the mortgage."

"Our house?" I pulled my hair back into a tight ponytail and then let it drop back onto my shoulders. "We're mortgage-free right now, Dave. That took a long while and a lot of hard work, you know." I could hear my voice rising.

"True." Dave took a deep breath.

"It's not like we're thirty."

"I know." His soft blue eyes locked on mine.

"The farm would be called Hillsborough Stables?" I said. I could feel my resistance softening.

He smiled. "Yes. The long-term plan would factor in Derrick and Darlene. They would have the option of buying the property—for fair market value—once the lease ran out." He looked away, as if considering what to say next, then met my gaze again. "We'd be tight financially for the first handful of years, but in the long run, it would be a sound investment."

"Yeah. I guess," I said. The "are you nuts?" conversation wasn't bubbling to the surface, yet I knew this farm idea held more than a hint or two of craziness.

"You know we're better at saving when we're focused on the debt, Renata. It's a good opportunity."

I nodded. No anger. No frustration. I couldn't seem to muster the emotions to articulate a protest. There was only calm. I didn't even recognize myself. Was this the new me?

"The time is right," Dave said.

"I know, the lease is up soon in Millgrove."

We stopped talking. The breeze blowing in through the patio door made the kitchen smell clean and fresh. Both cats had their noses pushed against the screen to check out a bird on the deck.

Suddenly, to throw Dave off, I announced in a menacing tone: "I only have one thing to say." I pursed my lips. Dave looked startled. "This is all Albert's fault... and Lusi, Magic, Lido, Pan, and Shorty's." I grinned and reached out for a hug. "This is nuts."

Not long after, we struck a deal, and presto—Dave and I owned a farm.

And yes, I realized, this was definitely the new me. This wasn't Dave seeing the decision one way and me seeing it another way, like in the past. This time was different. In an instant, I'd chosen something unthinkable and taken a new path *with* Dave to become farm owners and landlords. This time I didn't have to calculate, jot down the pros and cons, ruminate, or craft the other side of the argument. It was for the horses. With the government on their hooves, I couldn't turn my back. I certainly didn't see this coming way back when we were first married. But then again, while life with Dave Lumsden was many things, it was never predictable or boring.

A late September closing date gave us time to get our house appraised and sell things down by the lake.

That night, in the darkness of the bedroom, I went back to the beginning of our cottage adventure. Silently, I asked myself how I felt about moving on from the Lake Erie chapter in our lives. Year after year, nobody in the family— not my parents, sisters, or cousins—had taken a liking to cottage life. It wasn't surprising with my Italian heritage and Dave's Scottish background, since we hadn't grown up with a cottage. We always came up with a plethora of made-up excuses for not spending time at the lake: busy work lives, driving distance, poor summer weather, and a shortage of time off.

And yet, staring at the red glow of the alarm clock, I found I still had to come to terms with listing the properties. I remembered Dave touting the cottage investment shortly after we moved to Ancaster. In 2006 Dave had taken a new job with a construction and heavy equipment business, and we'd moved back to the Hamilton area. With Dave's withdrawn pension in hand, he proclaimed the best investment was earth. He suggested we invest the funds in a cottage on nearby Lake Erie. A sound idea, it took the present into consideration but also factored in our future. Besides, the prospect of looking at real estate appealed to the home-and-garden junkie in me.

We found a quintessential lakefront cottage, built in 1996 and located forty-five minutes from Ancaster, that just needed some fresh eyes and some loving. The bungalow cottage became ours in April. That summer we offered it up to family and friends, welcoming young, old, babies, and dogs.

Later that same year in August, the lakefront property next door went up for sale. A storey and a half, the neighbouring cottage sat on a lot similar in size to ours, but that's where the similarity ended.

Since becoming cottage owners, we'd noticed that the one next door stood quietly empty. We had affectionately nicknamed the dilapidated old eyesore "The Shit Shack." Built in the 1950s, the place had been forgotten by its aging owners, now octogenarians, according to the other lakeside neighbours.

Prone to worrywart tendencies, I thought about the "For Sale" sign and fretted over potential buyers and the level of noise they might subject us to.

"What are we going to do?" I asked Dave.

"Leave it with me," he said, and he called the listing agent. The best way to control noise was to become our own neighbour. The deal closed in September—only five months after we'd purchased the first cottage.

Season after season, Dave and I tried our best, and mostly failed, to get down to the lake. One thing always led to another, and despite being winterized, the cute cottage sat empty most weekdays and weekends.

Now, lying in bed, I pondered our impending huge new debt—the fieldstone-house-and-ninety-six-rolling-acres farm purchase. It made sense to move on from the lake—although even with money from the cottages, we would need to use some emergency savings and then take out the largest possible mortgage with the bank on our home to cover the substantial shortfall.

Within a few days of its debut on MLS, the dilapidated cottage sold for nearly full asking price and closed within a week. The other cottage sold two weeks later—the buyer of the old eyesore next door saw the potential and also bought the little lakefront bungalow. The closing date was suggested with the offer. To our surprise, the purchaser just happened to pick the same date we were taking possession of the farm. Perhaps, I thought, things were meant to be.

It felt more than a little crazy to think how much the direction of our lives had changed since Albert had entered the world. As cheesy as it might sound, I believed that once a person decided where they wanted to be, the path leading there became more obvious. The hardest part lay in figuring out the end point. Six months earlier, Dave and I never thought farm ownership was in our future, let alone financially possible. But we wanted Lusi, Albert, and the others to have a secure home. The horses were at the heart of our leap of faith. So yes, call it sentimentality gone insane, but all of it happened because we loved the horses. It dawned on me that I hadn't even seen the farm. What if I hated it? What if Lusi and Albert hated it too?

Chapter 10

THE RIGHT
REAL ESTATE

I wasn't able to actually set foot on the farm until a week before the closing date, but better late than never. Dave and I set out on the Queen Elizabeth Highway and then headed north.

Before long, Mohawk Raceway announced itself in the distance with flashing coloured lights. Not far from the well-known harness-racing A-track lay the small town of Moffat. At a four-way stop, I watched a crowd of cyclists gather at a bakery called Dar's Delights. From there we turned up First Line toward the farm.

As a couple, we'd moved a handful of times and owned a number of primary dwellings, plus the cottages. Real estate was simply real estate, right? I wasn't prepared for my gut reaction to the farm. More than once that day, I felt like an observer of the entire process rather than a participant. It was as if I were watching life through someone else's eyes. Yet as much as it all seemed surreal—I was experiencing an almost floating, hazy feeling—it was real.

Renata Lumsden

I hadn't expected Stonegate to be as amazing as it was, because looks on paper can be deceiving. Everyone I'm sure at some point in their life has had a particular building or piece of land affect them on a whole other level. In my case, the minute we turned onto the property, the farm spoke to me.

Stones scrunched under the car tires as we pulled up the drive. Rolling paddocks, laced together by what looked like an army of old-fashioned wooden soldiers holding hands, circled the barn up ahead and continued beside the house on the hill. A thick forest spread out beyond the century-old residence with an unending mix of greens, browns, and golds, like a peacock in full-feathered display. We parked on a slope, midway between the barn and house.

The towering trees whispered as warm air blew across my face. Surprisingly, it smelled fresher than any air in my recent memory. Built in the 1830s, the fieldstone house with its bright red door appeared to beckon me to enter. Instead, I circled the house and noticed three separate entrances. Seating areas and nooks were nestled around antique screened storm doors at the front, back, and side.

Dave pointed out the foundations of a former outbuilding behind the house. It had been dismantled and the fieldstones reused to create a terrace, which overlooked one of the paddocks. The previous owners were present and mentioned that they'd found numerous coloured glass bottles when they excavated. The finished product was a restful spot overlooking a stretch of stunning farm country dotted with contentedly grazing horses.

Looking out across the land, I had trouble connecting the view to the idea of actually owning a farm. I could sense my old self, pre-Albert's survival, trying to poke through the moment and cost out what ownership would mean. The farm and property felt right on another level, so I redoubled my efforts to prevent that old self from reappearing. Dave took me inside.

"You like it?" Dave said.

"I do. I could live here," I said, as I stood in the kitchen beside the stone fireplace. My eyes darted around. Old, buttery wood floors blended nicely with newer forest-green cabinets. I looked up at the soaring ceilings and then out one of two large, open sash windows. The drapes gently tapped the wall. "I'm sure Derrick and Darlene will enjoy many happy years in this place. It feels cozy."

"I agree." Dave smiled.

"Being surrounded by horses gives the place an even warmer feeling," I said. Sitting on the deep windowsill facing the yard, I could barely make out the road in the distance. Only the sounds of birds and insects filled my ears, which allowed me to think more clearly. I thought about Albert and Lusi, and how a couple of horses had taken me places I'd never dreamed of emotionally and were about to transform my life again.

On our way out, Dave stopped to chat with the farm owners and our agent. Meanwhile, I snuck down the gravel drive. Up close, the rectangular wooden barn with its metal roof looked bigger and sturdier than in the agent's brochure. After a couple of attempts and a bit more effort, I managed to pull open the barn door. A big grey horse with bright eyes stared at me. I knew a horse could signal anything it needed to communicate. This one's ears flicked forward and he nickered. I'd found a friend.

On Monday, September 29—just over eight months after Albert entered the world—we officially became farm owners. Darlene's parents moved into the fieldstone house right away. Her dad made sure things worked fine while her mom kept an eye on farm happenings and the gardens. Derrick, Darlene, and the entire Hillsborough crew would be moved over by December first. Neither horse nor human, though, would be completely settled at the farm—nor would the business be fully functional—until the new construction was completed at the end of March.

Immediately following possession, Dave made sure the proper paperwork was drawn up and the forms signed toward permits. We were about to build both a training arena and a second barn. Darlene and Derrick seemed nervous but excited at the prospect of starting anew. I felt excited too, but scared.

In early October, Pan and Shorty came back home. That day I was seized by a blend of excitement and concern. Shorty had lived at Ridgewood Farm for eight years and Pan for nearly four. I hoped they would be okay with the change of scenery. Always a good communicator, Darlene reported that Pan and Shorty arrived safely and were both "nice boys." The two horses were in good health overall, but their manes and tails had been cut short, likely due to excessive burrs, and they were in desperate need of a farrier. Darlene vowed to get the two horses looking pretty again soon.

I texted Darlene.

Pan's the Man.

She chimed in quickly.

Shorty too.

That night before bed, I gave thanks for Pan and Shorty's safe arrival.

The next day, Derrick sent us a single photo. Surrounded by a misty morning ground fog, the two horses stood grazing alone in a distant, sloping paddock. The sun, barely over the horizon, cast a soft blue-gold glow in the background. This serene image of Pan and Shorty relaxed my shoulders.

Now, with the return of the fifteen-year-old geldings, our horse holdings at Hillsborough Stables had expanded to five. We also found out that Mach Magic would be joining Lusi,

Lido, Albert, Pan, and Shorty. Magic needed a break from training due to the discovery of a small hairline fracture in her left front leg. It simply needed time to heal. The plan for her included stall rest and then reassessment in February.

"Magic was just starting to figure out the harness-race game," Dave said. He rubbed his face with both hands.

"I know. The timing isn't the best." I gave him a half smile. Dinner was nearly ready.

"No horses racing, and excavation for the barn and arena is held up in permits." He sighed.

"Hey. I cashed in a bunch of Air Miles and picked up gift cards for gas and coffee. We can eat, drink, and drive for a while on those," I said, trying to add something positive.

The new build delay was a rake in the road we didn't need. In the meantime, a retrofit of the existing barn got going.

"All we can do is hold on tight and enjoy the ride," Dave said, and he took a big bite of his grilled cheese sandwich.

"I hope you like the new austerity measures in my meal planning. It's all Albert's fault, you know," I said, just as the ketchup bottle made a silly squirting sound. I could only laugh. It was either laugh, I thought, or cry. Because now, on the back nine of life, Dave and I had bought a horse farm because of our preemie and were plunging deep into debt.

Chapter 11

TAKING A LEAP

After ten years in Millgrove, Darlene and Derrick moved a little over thirty-five kilometres to Moffat. On November 29 and 30, they had a very busy weekend shipping horses.

I stood back with Dave, and from a safe distance under a tree we watched the equine wave come in. Moving day for humans could be chaotic, but moving dozens of horses took things to a new level of interesting. I had no idea how it was going to go. My ears were filled with joyful sounds.

Lusi seemed as happy as a two-year-old filly. With wild snorts she took off as if chasing the starter's car and whipped across the new paddock, neighing as she paced. Like a champion, she won the imaginary race and finally came to rest, burying her nose in the grass. I called her name and she ignored me. Instead, Lusi bit and tore up huge mouthfuls before she took off once again to another, yet unexplored section of paddock. *Rip, rip, rip* went the sound she made. I imagined that the brownish November grass still tasted sweet and good in this unfamiliar place. Energized, she couldn't seem to get enough of the sweeping fresh air and satisfying grass. Then all of a sudden, Lusi stopped.

"What's she doing now?" I gave Dave a look. He just shrugged.

We watched.

Down she went in the wettest, muddiest patch of dirt. Rolling from side to side between the wiry damp grass and patches of mud, Lusi let out great whinnies of joy.

"She's something else," I said.

Dave laughed. "Isn't she, though."

Maybe she'd already forgotten the trailer ride and Millgrove, her retirement home for the past five years? Watching her kick her legs in the air, I felt relief. At this early juncture it seemed that Lusi approved.

Now a cool wind blew down from the north. Empty horse trailers pulled away as the last animal was safely unloaded. The sun started to set. Meandering clouds cast long shadows across the landscape, signalling that the time had come for the horses to retreat to the barn. We headed home.

According to Derrick and Darlene, once inside the sturdy wooden stable, our domineering matriarch's contented demeanour changed. They sent us reports throughout the evening.

A wild, ringing neigh shrilled from the stall at the far end of the shedrow. The accommodations seemed to throw Lusi into a state. The new arrangements lacked the spacious proportions of the double-size broodmare stall she'd grown accustomed to. She ran her teeth along the boards and kicked the walls. The ruckus made the structure vibrate. From stalls nearby, a dozen heads turned with eyes wide. Lusi seemed to be protesting the inferior lodgings of the single box stall adjacent to a parked tractor. She let Derrick and Darlene know that the queen of the barn was not impressed.

For an entire week, our big bay mare chewed on the middle-stall wallboards as if a daily supply of wood shavings would magically expand the space's dimensions. It wasn't until Derrick used a special concoction of cayenne pepper and water on the area that Lusi finally stopped acting like a broad-tailed, tree-gnawing rodent.

I thought about Lusi's new wood-eating habits and her rowdy, thundering thwacks against the walls. As a racehorse, she was known to be moody. Many of the good ones had that kind of temperament. Even as a broodmare, she'd had her bitchy moments with the other mares and with Darlene. I'd hoped that Lusi's sour mood would soon pass. After all, we'd taken this leap with our mare's best interests and future in mind. So much was on the line.

Meanwhile, the weanlings, Albert, Chester, and the others, including Rodeo and Sailor—both bay, and both rather gangly—were settling. They cropped grass peacefully and got acquainted with their new domain.

Dave and I often stopped by the farm. Upon seeing us, Albert would kick his heels sideways while dancing and running along the fence line. With mane and tail flying, he'd let out little whinnies of joy.

Everything horse and human surrounding the relocation from Millgrove to Moffat seemed to go well—until Derrick sent word of an incident. From his descriptions, I felt as if I'd been there to witness it.

While exploring the paddock with his buddies, Albert must have been taken with the ridge in the distance. Always one to be a little bit curious and somewhat of a discipline problem at times, our boy wandered from the pack. As he moved up the hill, he got closer to the farmhouse. From his position, he must have heard the voice of buddy Derrick and the bark of pal Oscar. The colt continued to climb higher and higher and closer and closer. At the top of the ridge, a small fence and steep embankment halted Albert's ascent. Eyeing the obstacle, the young horse likely stretched his head high and sniffed the fence laterals, trying to craft a plan to get over the fence. Then Albert tackled the obstacle—or it tackled him.

Derrick told us that our boy somehow managed to thread both front feet and his large head through the fence. Almost immediately, Albert would have realized he was in trouble. He must have wiggled and shifted and snorted and bucked, but no movement brought any release.

In the meantime, the pack of weanlings down below began running in circles. With noses lifted to the sky, they neighed for their compromised friend. The winds carried their call. Suddenly, Oscar appeared on the ridge high above. The boxer barked and barked.

Derrick came running. "What's going on?" The dog's gaze continued uninterrupted. Following Oscar's stare, Derrick noticed the distressed horse. "It's okay, Albert. I'll be right there!" Derrick shouted. He took off toward the garage workshop, and Oscar ran along with him.

In the workshop Derrick grabbed what tools he needed and hurried to the parked Gator. Oscar jumped into the passenger seat. With one hand on the dog's collar, Derrick revved the engine and the pair took off.

With the paddock gate securely closed behind them, man and man's best friend sped past half a dozen horses, their ears twitching at the fast-moving vehicle.

Through the window, Darlene told us, she noticed Oscar and Derrick zoom by. Unpacking yet another bunch of boxes, she dropped the towels she had just discovered and dashed out the front door. Darlene shouted after Derrick, but the roar of the motor drowned her out. Seeing them go through the paddock gate, she took off for the stone deck behind the house. She watched the Gator race across the paddock.

The vehicle buzzed and bumped along, causing the young colts to scatter. Derrick had wrapped his right arm around

Oscar, and he held the dog low against the seat just before he veered up the hill where Albert had drifted. On the incline, weeds and low-hanging branches whooshed and thumped against the front fender and the wheel wells. Derrick and Oscar pushed forward. Eyeing the terrain ahead, Derrick navigated around gnarled tree roots until he and the Gator were nearly on top of the young horse.

Albert's hind legs jerked his back end. His muscles stretched and bulged. Derrick cut the engine and the colt let out a loud neigh. Derrick told us he saw blood run between Albert's eyes and down his nose from his open wounds.

Darlene shouted from her vantage point, "Need any help?"

"Nope." Derrick waved the sledgehammer in the air. "I'm all set." It was the tool of choice for breaking rocks or, in this case, knocking apart fences. Derrick walked over and knelt down beside Albert. With both hands holding the tool, he showed the foal the heavy metal and wood device. Albert sniffed it. "Hey buddy," Derrick said, in a calm tone. "I'm going to give this fence a whack and get you out." He demonstrated in a rehearsal-like fashion. "Got it?"

The horse's eyes were liquid and large. Derrick pushed down gently on the colt's neck, wound up, and gave the fence a good smash. Albert stayed still. Derrick gave the board one final smack. The length of timber let go, and the gap allowed Albert to nudge his head and legs free. The horse lifted his nose high and shook his mane.

Our boy's behaviour surprised everyone. It wasn't typical, but then again, nothing about Albert was typical. He'd always been curious, attention-seeking, and fearless. None of the other young ones had wandered. They all stayed put below the incline and enjoyed the expansive paddock. We just shook our heads.

Oscar barked at his newly freed friend while Derrick inspected Albert for injuries.

"How is he?" Darlene called out.

Derrick gave her the thumbs-up sign. Luckily, Albert had only a few shallow cuts. Derrick guided Albert in a small circle to be sure he was all right. "You'll be sore tomorrow," he said. He ruffled Albert's forelock, knowing that a few days of stall rest would allow the youngster to work out any stiffness. Derrick told us he kissed the velvet muzzle before coaxing the horse down the ridge to see his mates. Thank goodness our boy wasn't seriously injured. Oh, Albert!

Lusi was eating stall boards and now Albert was catching himself in fences. Albert, with his great bloodlines and potential, could have done some real damage to himself. And I still couldn't completely shake the feeling that his preemie issues might haunt us later. Albert and his mother were at the heart of our farm purchase, yet the newness of the relocation had them both acting up. In Albert's case, his behaviour was dangerous. I crossed my fingers and hoped that time would settle things down as far as Lusi and her only son were concerned.

For Shorty and Pan, the move over to the new Hillsborough Stables in Moffat was the pair's second in two months. Like a parent, I worried. But like children, they adapted.

Pan and Shorty didn't race anymore, and as geldings they couldn't breed, so there was no possibility they would ever have offspring in the racing limelight. However, I, Dave, and everyone else were thrilled to have the boys stalled so close by again—Ridgewood Farm had meant a four-hour-plus return trip. Now we could see Pan and Shorty whenever we journeyed to our farm. On each visit—and there were numerous—the two boys heard Dave's familiar voice and sauntered over for treats and a welcome pat. Eventually they seemed to remember me and accept my presence too. It warmed everyone's heart to see the retirees alongside young Lido, Magic, and Albert, and all our horses get a good home.

The joy of having Pan and Shorty back with us overshadowed my financial concerns most days. I understood that the geldings were two extra mouths to feed that would never earn again. Too bad they weren't at their racing prime, I thought. Our expanding herd numbers stuck in my mind as the farm construction project finally took off.

During the new barn and arena build, with all its uncertainty surrounding time and cost, Dave and I talked and talked. Long conversations over the dinner table seemed to help keep the anxiety and stress from bubbling up to an unmanageable level. Neither of us brought up details about the bills or our sad bank balance. There was no need to dwell on the obvious. Instead, we'd speak about our horses, past, present, and future. We were just two people who loved each other—and now we had the love of horses and harness racing in common.

"Remember when I owned Lusi with a partner?" Dave said. "I still can't believe he wanted to sell her at the Harrisburg auction. I'm so glad I bought out his half, even though I knew we were taking a chance."

"We were—come to think of it, we went out on a financial limb back then too. But we knew she was special." I leaned forward. Mesmerized for several seconds by the candlelight through my water glass, I felt myself float to a more even emotional keel. Lusi and the other horses had a way of doing that to me.

Back then, over ten years ago at Harrisburg, there had been plenty of potential buyers looking for a great mare like our Lusi: horse people from far and wide, drifting stall to stall, eyeballing each specimen with the same intensity with which investigators evaluate crime scenes. If she had gone to that auction, we would have lost her for sure.

Dave reached for my hand. "And now we own a farm because of our mare and her foals."

I looked up and caught his eye. "Mach Magic reminds me most of Lusi," I said. "Although she's missing one of her mom's back white socks."

Dave nodded. "Magic's a beauty, with talent like her mom."

"True, but I'm nervous about that hairline fracture."

"The time off to rest her joints will help." Dave scooped up the last few bits of scrambled eggs on his plate.

"I hope so," I said, but I was thinking, *What if it doesn't? What if we end up with another non-racing mouth to feed?*

"Some race as two-year-olds and others at the age of three," Dave said. "She'll make it."

On the outside, everything measured up for Magic at a little more than 16 hands high. She wasn't a biter and didn't snake her beautiful head or pin her ears. In fact, I'd never met a horse with such a balanced blend of looks, demeanour, and mechanical stability—she had the right angles in the right places, known in the horse world as "good conformation." Surprisingly, though, it took a while for Magic to be ready "to go" out on the track. As a three-year-old, after time off to heal her leg, she started out okay. But, green on the inside, she needed time for her mind to mature and put together all the parts and pieces of harness racing and competition.

Ted MacDonnell, her trainer after Travis, told us he liked Magic's athleticism and, more importantly, how she felt when he sat behind her in the jog cart. He'd been fooled before, but he thought she could be a winner.

He and his groom, Shawna, were as close to our big filly as anyone could be. Shawna had been around horses for decades. Solid and sinewy with a sexy, throaty voice and luminous blonde hair, she was petite and thin by groom standards. But by people standards, she packed the uncanny strength and agility to handle any size mare, filly, colt, or gelding under her care. I often watched her work and wondered if one day I could be as confident as she was around the horses, despite my slight stature.

Magic didn't seem to like much. Maybe a few neck scratches were okay, and she enjoyed carrots and of course peanut butter bars. Like her mother, the headstrong missy had to have things her own way. The change of the seasons bothered the horse too, especially springtime. With the release of pollen came Magic's allergies. As with Lusi, mucus would appear in her nostrils during training-mile workouts and disturb her breathing. A post-training scope showed more mucus in her throat.

Horse allergy management required the correct combination of medications and stall bedding from spring right through to summer. Once Ted figured out how to treat Magic's seasonal allergies, she really took off on the track. On May 4, Ted's eyes grew wide with excitement: she posted a training-mile time of 2:02 seconds—he told us he knew the young horse was getting close to racing.

Three weeks later, the time had finally arrived for Mach Magic to qualify at the track. Success in the qualifying races would allow the mare to compete for purse money as a fully fledged racehorse. Ted and Shawna loaded her up and trucked to Mohawk Raceway. I sat back watching from the grandstand. No one else was around. I knew that one or two reasonable performances here and she'd be ready for real racing. I could hardly breathe as the field took off. With the wind in Magic's mane and her neck stretched for the finish line, she raced in 1:56.3 seconds, with the last quarter mile at a speedy 26.3 seconds. I sprang to my feet and cheered out loud for our girl and the surprisingly good qualifying show.

Qualifiers weren't nearly as reliable or important as real races, but the stopwatch didn't lie. I knew what it meant. The timed result suggested that Mach Magic was ready to face her competition and beat some mares out there. One of

Lusi's foals was finally on the verge of competition. With any luck she might help earn her keep too, I thought, and lessen at least one financial strain.

The summer of 2015 arrived. The new barn and arena were fully functional. The construction end of the project was more or less behind us, and my writing efforts had produced something resembling a book. Episodes of doubt about the writing and our money situation still came and went. Sometimes they cropped up once or twice a day, and other times, if I was sleep deprived or frustrated with work, they flooded my thoughts every ten minutes. Those days I retreated to bed early. A good sleep always seemed to help bring a better perspective.

The cost of the new training arena and barn didn't exactly unfold as planned. The scope of the project turned out to be much bigger than we'd ever contemplated. The original quote from the builder was far from turnkey, and finishing costs over the winter had piled up, mainly because of unforeseen variables caused by Mother Nature. February was the coldest month recorded since 1875, and when it wasn't bitterly cold, it was always snowing.

In the end, the project cost far more than the $70,000 Dave and I had talked about. We'd come to the 70K figure when we were thinking of one small barn (the arena was always going to be an added expense). But we underestimated how big the barn needed to be once the spacious broodmare stalls were factored into the equation, along with laundry facilities, a wash stall, an office, and storage space. Everything combined sent the total ballooning to *ten times* the original figure in our minds.

In the old days I would have gone into a full-on-shouting-with-hands-waving panic, and the pad of paper would have joined us at the dinner table. The new Renata merely took a few deep breaths. Full-time work commitments helped keep

Renata Lumsden

our minds off the finances and kept the funds coming in, plus the farm rent money helped. That amount varied from month to month because of a unique twist in the arrangement. We paid Darlene and Derrick a fee to care for our horses. So depending how many of our herd were stalled at Hillsborough Stables at any given time, the value of the rent went up or down. Nevertheless, Dave and I never stopped believing we were on the right path despite the heaviness of our debt load. It was an investment, after all, we told ourselves, not a bet. A visit with Lusi, Albert, and all our horses always settled my nerves.

My writing also helped push away my concerns about our financial situation as well as feelings of uncertainty about my authorial abilities. The writing courses, a conference, and tons of how-to-write books from the local library had taken me further and helped improve my skills at a reasonable cost. Mentors appeared to spur me forward too. Janis, whom I met through a friend, seemed to materialize just when I felt like I was at a crossroads. An English teacher at the local elementary level, she had been writing her own memoir for a few years. On her suggestion, we exchanged manuscripts.

Janis used a red pen on my stuff and I loved it. More than a half-dozen exchanges took place. In a safe and non-threatening environment, these exchanges taught me so much, especially about punctuation. Her work was already well honed, in an *Angela's Ashes* sense—a book we'd both read and loved. I was grateful for the lessons and writing interaction, and thrilled because it was free. I wasn't too sure what Janis gained from me, although she seemed appreciative when I offered feedback.

Prior to working with Janis, *The Bounty of Illusionist* had ballooned to 120,000 words. Pairing with her and exchanging an equal number of pages each week allowed me to trim the manuscript way down. Another mentor of mine, an author named William Thomas who wrote in the pet and animal genre, had stressed that the word count for my book should max out at about 70,000 words. So when I got close to that number, I forced an ending with Janis's help and let go of a chain of chapters—perhaps for another book one day.

My writing, the herd, and Dave's faith in the farm allowed me to ride out the peak of our financial storm. In fact, my Zen-like feelings were strongest whenever Dave and I ventured out to Hillsborough. The individual personalities of our horses and their antics in the barn or paddock made us laugh. Two things became certain throughout the ups and downs: Dave and I were committed to each other, and Albert and all the horses were worth it.

In fact it occurred to me that, in my mind and heart, I was beginning to view our little herd not simply as beloved animals, but more like family members. I kept that thought to myself for now.

Chapter 12

TWO BIG WINS, TWO HUGE SHOCKS

It was June 2015. Mach Magic had drawn the four-hole post position at Mohawk. She was competing against a field of ten mares, including the likes of Glamour Seelster, So Raven, and Voodoo Charm, to name a few. Under the track lights, driver Jody Jamieson guided Mach Magic to a third-place finish. It marked the start of a run of top three finishes and some welcome racing luck for our mare.

From June to September, Mach Magic paced her way beyond our expectations in earnings. By the time the doors closed for Mohawk racetrack's annual shutdown, she had more than paid her way for the year. In fact, Mach Magic was on her way to covering not only herself financially, but also a couple of retired geldings and a matriarchal mare. Dave and I wondered how she would fare racing from October to December. We knew that when horses were feeling good, like Magic was, they liked to compete every ten days or so. Now the harness-racing schedule in Ontario shifted from Milton to Toronto. The arrival of the cool fall weather made us both smile; it was the perfect season for our big girl.

By the tail end of 2015, when other three-year-olds were taking time off from the track, Mach Magic was smack in the middle of her year-one racing peak because of the delay caused by the hairline fracture. The time had come at last, I thought, for our filly to get her chance at Woodbine Racetrack.

Going back to the big track in Toronto was surreal for Dave and me. It had taken exactly six years—from Lusi's racing career retirement to today—to reach Woodbine, the pinnacle of Standardbred racing, with one of her babies. Mach Magic was strong enough and talented enough to be there.

A haunting familiarity surrounded us, yet Lusi was missing. Somehow life had plotted out a new harness-racing trajectory for Dave and me, yet I couldn't imagine a different one. Rather than question or doubt our situation in that space and time, I stood beside Dave filled with a deep sense of trust. Trust that the next chapter in the horse story and our lives was emerging. This time Dave wasn't alone in recognizing it.

Like a couple of bobbleheads, we stared out at the track, back again at the grandstand, and then out again at the track. Flags whipped in the chilly wind.

"Let's hope the driver doesn't pull her back into the middle of the pack. She hates the pull-back move," Dave said. "She likes to pace to the front right off the gate."

"I know. Don't worry, Ted will tell the driver."

Dave rubbed both hands together. "My hands are freezing."

I grabbed his hands just as the speaker above us roared to life.

"Mach Magic, owned and bred by Dave Lumsden," said the announcer. Dave puffed up as our big bay filly passed by in the post parade with one white sock flashing. Magic, our homebred, wasn't an expensive horse compared to those purchased at auction south of the border. She was our baby, though, thanks to Dave's dedication to her mother.

Lusi's style had been to roll out like a stretch limousine—sleek, classy, and solid. But big girl Magic was more like a souped-up truck—she paced by us all-powerful and massive. The other difference I noticed between mother and daughter lay in Magic's striking facial features: she had an extraordinarily beautiful head.

The starting-gate car pulled away from the field. Two minutes later, it was all over.

Dave pumped his fist in the air. "Did you see that?" He grabbed me around the waist and hugged me off the ground.

I laughed out loud. "Yes!" Amazed, I was at a loss for words.

"She crushed the field," Dave said. "Our girl!"

Magic had floated to the front and run off with a commanding win in her first competition on the Toronto track. Dave and I whooped and cheered. One week later, Mach Magic took off in full pacing mode from gate to wire—and won again. The longer the Woodbine stretch drive at the finish, the more lengths she won by. Each race victory in Toronto lacked any of the common racing issues that could leave owners and the betting public upset. Shades of Lusi: when Magic won, she dominated.

Mach Magic, the daughter of Illusionist and Mach Three, had given both Dave and me goosebumps at Woodbine.

The purse winnings helped, and I noticed that Dave deposited both cheques the day they arrived by post. We'd made it through the first year of mountainous debt. Our relationship made it and the horses made it. My moments of panic and anxiety were becoming more like a simmer than a rolling boil. Patience wasn't something I'd been born with, but over time, along with Dave's calming influence and confidence about owning a farm, I was getting better at it.

Meanwhile, Albert was in a different situation than his older sister Magic.

Chester, Rodeo, Sailor, and the other weanlings had all left Hillsborough Stables. The boys—Albert and his friends—would turn two in January 2016. Their time to move into the awaiting arms of their first trainers had arrived. In the fall of 2015, Albert was the last to leave the farm. Often I'd wondered if this day would ever come.

Ted MacDonnell's trailer pulled up early on Thursday, November 5. The sun shone that afternoon. It was warm—the high was predicted to exceed 20 degrees Celsius. We all welcomed the unseasonably dry weather that sometimes occurs in autumn in Ontario. I considered it a good omen, excellent for transporting a horse.

I thought about Albert all day. Work commitments kept me from seeing him off. The midwives promised to take videos, and as usual, they were true to their word.

Sitting in my office, I pushed play. On the cell phone screen before me, a light breeze released a medley of brightly coloured leaves from nearby fruit trees. There was only silence as the videographer panned the landscape. The paddocks were full. Each grassy corral contained a single tall, sleek Thoroughbred or harness-racing competitor. Running and bucking with joyful exuberance, they were busy at the moment just being horses.

Now Derrick, followed by Oscar, entered the scene. Derrick pulled open the barn door. The video, on what must have been Darlene's phone, showed the horseman venturing inside.

"C'mon buddy, you gotta go with Ted and learn to race," Derrick said from the shedrow. Albert's massive head thrust through the stall-door opening. With more than forty horses at Hillsborough Stables, it was easy for one bay or brown to blur into another, sometimes even for the most seasoned horse person. Inevitably, however, a handful or more made an impression. Albert's size and spotted coat, combined with his personality, made him easy to recognize anywhere.

Oscar and his master entered Albert's stall. The dog's tail whipped back and forth.

Almost two years earlier, when equine and canine had met, Oscar was agile and full of energy. Now in his geriatric years and barely able to support his back end with failing hips, Oscar had walked over in a slow and tottery manner for one last goodbye.

Albert had entered Hillsborough Stables as a delicate bottle-fed foal. Today on the video, our boy ascended the trailer ramp as a strapping independent and energetic colt. Like his mother, Albert was powerful, with attitude and personality. Yet he retained an underlying sweetness from his early days surrounded by people. Approachable and friendly, he listened well to human commands.

I wasn't surprised when Albert followed orders and loaded onto the trailer like a veteran. Derrick secured the horse into place. They locked eyes. "You be a good boy and listen to Ted." He kissed Albert's muzzle and jumped down onto the gravel drive. Oscar let out two booming barks after the trailer door closed. Ted waved an arm out the truck window before he turned north onto First Line. I said a silent prayer for Albert and his journey to the big racing oval.

The road up to this point had been a winding one for Albert.

Change seemed to suit Albert, I thought, as I rewound the video and the horse's past mixed with ours in my thoughts. In Albert's short life, he'd shifted from the warmth of the animal hospital to the safe confines of his mother's side at Hillsborough Stables in Millgrove. Later in 2014, at the age of seven months, he was weaned with the other foals and moved to an independent stall. Late that same year, all of

Hillsborough Stables moved over to Moffat and their new home. There was much equine shuffling of quarters due to the new barn build, which lasted from January to April. In early spring 2015, Albert and his friends—the young boys, as they were called—moved outside to romp explore, graze, and play day and night.

I remembered running around in late May 2015 passing out treats among our small herd. My last stop was the yearling paddock. I'd saved enough carrots to keep the handful of young boys happy while I snuck Albert his granola bar. My rubber boots on the gravel didn't soften my approach. With ears pricked, a few of the horses had started in my direction. Chester's squiggly blaze and height made him easy to spot among the gang pushing toward me. Then I noticed the other big colt, with the grey stitching of hair across his nose. I called out.

"Albert! Albert!"

His ears swivelled and he picked up the pace. The others were closing fast. On tiptoes, I reached as far as possible over the electric fence. Just as my boy grabbed the treat, something strange caught my eye. I felt the blood rush out of my face and I stood staring, unable to move.

Sitting in my office now, remembering that day, I shuddered. The sight still felt so real in my mind, I made the sign of the cross.

Back then, a hair-covered lump the size of a fist bulged on the outside of Albert's right front leg. Just above the knee joint, the mass sat firmly attached. Sunlight bounced off the lump's bay-coloured contours as the horse jostled in between his friends. In the momentary shadows, darkness masked its huge proportions and made me wonder if I'd imagined it. I shifted positions from standing to crouched, making sure I hadn't mistaken a chunk of mud or poop for the unusual brown bulge.

Once certain that the growth was real, I recovered my medical instincts. I jumped in fast, determined, and fearless. Reaching between fence laterals, I ran my hand along Albert's leg while keeping up a soft, distracting chatter. I only managed to grip the mass for a few seconds. Each time I tried again to touch it, Albert pulled away. I wondered if it caused him pain, although with his ears forward in a sign of curiosity and interest, he looked untroubled. But he definitely didn't want me to touch the lump again. A wave of questions came crashing down in my mind.

How long had the lump been there? Could it be cancerous? Why hadn't I noticed it sooner? Had anyone else noticed it? Why didn't any of the others have similar lumps?

I tried to wrap my head around what I was seeing. I urgently wanted to understand how the lump had grown under my attentive nose. Dave and I saw Albert on a regular basis, so maybe we weren't noticing the details. Plus, our boy moved within a group of young animals, which meant we didn't often see Albert standing apart from the others, especially when we offered treats each visit.

Right there I lost it. I shoved the remaining carrot slices at the boys and turned and ran toward the barn.

"Darlene! Derrick!" I shouted up and down the shedrows. Silence. Only calm brown eyes and perky ears greeted me.

Less than a week later, Albert had surgery.

Shortly after Albert arrived at the equine medical centre, we got a call. Some additional unusual contours on the horse's hind legs had the vet's attention. They asked if we'd give the okay to take X-rays of both of Albert's back legs. We gave permission via email, and within less than an hour the digital images showed up.

Captured in the black-and-white pictures were multiple large, round bits of mineralized debris surrounded by stringy material. The lump I'd noticed sat on Albert's right elbow, but that wasn't all. The vets found the same bony, pulpy combinations in the opposite leg, in the left stifle area. Multiple views of the lump and other areas at various angles revealed what looked like a hardened bunch of white grapes. Their presence represented the possibility of a multitude of disease processes, from something very serious to nothing at all, with localized trauma at the heart of things. At first I had trouble grasping the trauma part. Then the doctors suggested that Albert's previous history as a neonatal foal—lying down instead of being upright and moving about on all four legs—was the most likely cause.

The bony growths were present over Albert's joints, pressure points, and bony prominences that had rested in contact with the ground. The diagnosis was calcinosis circumscripta.

The day Albert was diagnosed, time seemed to halt momentarily as I read and reread the texts from Dave. In the messages, he praised the vets for coming up with a diagnosis, reassured me that Albert was where he needed to be for care, and told me everything would work out. I appreciated his "cup half full" spin but needed to know more. In an effort to better understand the etiology of the disease, I grabbed some nearby radiographic pathology textbooks from my office bookshelf and started Googling things on my phone. I flew between horse-related data on the internet and the human medical textbooks. Would Albert's disease affect his quality or quantity of life? Or both? I felt sick.

Calcinosis circumscripta—irregularly shaped calcified deposits that formed within a fibrous tissue capsule—reportedly developed in young, growing horses. Surgical removal was the only treatment available and carried a good prognosis. I'd read that some owners considered the disease more of a simple cosmetic barnacle than a worrisome mole. The condition wasn't often associated with lameness or shortening of the animal's lifespan. I wondered if the bony armies would become less dense and widespread after Albert matured.

I thought about his precarious start to life. The room felt hot. This new twist set off more alarm bells for me about Albert's ability to participate in harness racing. Unlike his champion mother, who could be a moody creature at times and tolerated very little, Albert was different. Albert had always been different. The horse could stand absolutely still and let me run my hands all over him. In his body language, I heard "I trust you." In his eyes, I saw "I love you." Albert had all the instincts of a regular racehorse mixed in with the charm of a loving pet. With the diagnosis, I wondered if he'd be able to move along—jogging, training, and racing—like all the other colts his age. I was filled with serious doubts, but I kept my thoughts to myself.

Following surgery for the lump, Albert returned home to Hillsborough Stables. The surgeon left the mineral deposits on his left leg alone because they were smaller and closer to nearby joints. With his stitched-up right leg, the colt was on stall rest combined with hand-walking. Inside the new barn, Albert had secured prime real estate near the entrance. All the post-surgical horses got the stall closest to Darlene's office. When we arrived for our first visit since his return, Albert poked his massive head out the "V" opening, nosily checking out Dave and me and his surroundings. Once in a while, he got a little nip from his neighbour—mother Lusi was stalled right next to her son. We laughed when we saw it. The sight of the two of them, poking their heads out side by side, made me smile despite the misspelling of Lusi's stick-on stall nameplate. The *I Love Lucy* version of her name was so common that I couldn't bring myself to point it out yet again and spoil the moment. Instead, I took a close-up with my phone—laughing more heartily to keep down the mild irritation inside.

"Hi, buddy." I reached out and stroked Albert's neck and muzzle. His scent lifted into the air. His coat smelled intoxicating, even with a slight medicinal odour from the surgery.

Meanwhile, Lusi had Dave's attention. The mare's tongue was flapping, granola crumbs stuck in her whiskers.

Suddenly Darlene burst out of her office. "I found Albert lying on his bad side this morning." She shook her head in a huff of frustration.

"Guess that doesn't help." I nodded in sympathy. Apparently, Darlene had changed Albert's bandages earlier only to find his incision wide open.

"Oh, Albert!" Darlene ran a hand over her face. "This means a house call, you know." She turned, her cell phone in her other hand. "And believe me, Albert"—she waved her finger—"you won't be impressed!" She put her phone to her ear and trailed off down the shedrow.

The vet arrived, cleaned up the wound edges, and restitched things into place. "In ten to twelve days the stiches can come out," he said.

"Provided Albert keeps them in that long," Darlene added.

"Granular tissue should form and close things up," said the vet.

Darlene was charged with flushing the wound and changing the bandage while keeping an eye on new flesh forming. In her words: "It'll be fine. Maybe a scar but not too bad."

My mind raced as we drove down First Line on our way back to Ancaster. This, I realized, was what the parents of neonates must go through. The fact that our baby had health issues requiring surgery fuelled an already-present cloud of concern in my mind for our boy's future. Even if everything healed up, would Albert be able to use his legs for serious, high-impact racing?

A few weeks after Albert's operation, I stopped by the farm on my way to Mohawk Raceway. The setting sun's crimson veil covered the barn. I pulled in and parked. I'd have the place all to myself, I thought, and ran inside.

I was barely through the barn entrance when Lusi started her show. Like an actor in a well-rehearsed play, she flicked her ears forward at the sound of my plastic bag. Her eyes grew alert and she moved closer to the stall door. Lusi pawed playfully, first with her right leg and then with her left. Before I reached her, she'd dug through her shavings all the way to the black rubber mat on the floor of her stall. "Hey, stop that," I said sharply. Lusi continued, and then threw her head up and down as if trying to speed up the delivery of the treat. I was used to the rude horse behaviour. Good stable manners weren't something Dave and I knew enough about to put much time or effort into reinforcing with our herd. Unfortunately, they all pawed.

Upon hearing the crackle of the plastic wrapper, Albert tossed his head out on cue.

"Your turn next, buddy." I ripped open the first package. My big bay mare nearly kissed me while I fed her a granola bar. Lusi had been particularly agreeable since her son had taken up residence beside her. Meanwhile, Albert enjoyed the sliced carrots I'd brought followed by his granola treat. I peeked over the stall door beyond Albert's massive head at the bandage. Everything looked well secured.

Moving down the row, I heard Lido before I found her. *Bang. Bang. Bang.* Then the rattle of metal filled the air. The profile of her nose caught my eye. The wooden door of her stall bulged—straining the looped chain locking mechanism—with the force of her chest and legs against it. As soon as I reached Lido's stall, she retreated inside. "Hey. Don't play timid with me," I said. The only one of Lusi's offspring not to take a liking to granola bars, Lido enjoyed more than a few handfuls of the sliced carrots I offered her. She quickly backed away into the stall with her nose down once the food was gone. One more stop and then I'd rush off to the track. I hurried across the gravel drive and up the familiar incline. The two boys met me at the paddock gate. Pan and Shorty gobbled down the last of my carrot slices and inhaled one granola snack I divided between them.

Within ten minutes, I was walking across the full parking lot at Mohawk racetrack. It was nice to be back racing in Milton. The late evening sky had turned into a patchwork of pink, white, and blue. An added slight breeze was perfect for racing. Dressed in a light jacket and scarf, I enjoyed the fresh air and cool temperatures. Once inside, I headed straight for the wagering window—ten dollars to win and place on Mach Magic. Bursting through the back doors of the grandstand, I noticed her one white sock as the mare paced by me during her warm-up. Race five's final results flashed across the giant electronic tote board. I looked at my watch. Her race wouldn't go off for more than an hour.

It was summer 2015. The track was bathed in the last light of dusk, which somehow intensified the colours of the scene around me. A nearby weathered wooden picnic table held a small contingent of patrons, their noses buried in their race programs. I suppressed the urge to strike up a conversation and brag about my girl—perhaps they were owners as well and we were competing in the same race. The crowd was thick. Young, old, male, female, their faces were alight with broad smiles against tanned cheeks.

I waved over the fence and wished Shawna and Ted good luck before the start.

Ted gave me the thumbs-up signal. "Where's Dave?"

I cupped my hands around my mouth. "He's at a dinner meeting."

I paced and waited, enjoying the races and the energy all around me.

"One minute. One minute to post," blared through the racetrack loudspeakers.

The time had finally come. The horses lined up pacing and the starter's car pulled away. They were off! Mach Magic got away in fourth. After a short breather, she pulled out first over on the outside and settled into first along the rail. Coming for home, I could see her giving it her all. Late in the final eighth of the mile, she veered out a bit away from the rail. Voodoo Charm snuck into the gap. "Mach Magic held on safely for second," said the announcer. The driver let our girl jog well beyond the backstretch barn entrance and finish her race.

I texted Dave.

She came second!

He texted back with all emoji symbols—two hearts and a kiss.

Walking back to the car with my head held high, I felt the breeze brush my cheeks. I oozed pride of ownership in the first of Lusi's progeny to make it to the track and carry on her racing legacy. Albert's disease and subsequent surgery, the new barn and arena build, the farm debt, they all got shuffled to the back of my thoughts. The smile stayed on my face all the way home.

I had no idea what was coming next.

A few days later, Dave came home and dropped his keys and wallet on the counter. "Darlene just called," he said.

When my eyes met his, I could see something in his face. "What is it?"

"The vet's calling soon. Shorty Bones is in the hospital." What was left of the colour drained from his face. "It's colic."

"Oh shit." I knew twisted bowel had almost done in Lido as a two-year-old, and herniation during her pregnancy with Albert had threatened Lusi. Bowel issues could be debilitating and cause death if left untreated.

"Shorty didn't want to board the trailer," Dave said. "The horse kept looking back at Pan. Darlene thought Shorty knew he might not be coming back." His lip quivered.

"Why would she say that?" I could hear my own voice rising, so I took a deep breath.

"Darlene doesn't mean anything by it," Dave said. "She hasn't had much luck with colic cases after surgery."

I sat at the kitchen table I'd just set for dinner. "What are Shorty's symptoms?"

Dave pulled up a chair. "He wasn't his usual Shorty Bones prankster self. He seemed depressed. He wasn't mauling Derrick as usual at feed time."

We both stared off into space. I gazed out the patio door beyond my loving husband's shoulder, while Dave looked up at the wall of cabinets behind me.

The ringing of Dave's cell phone jolted us.

"You won't know until you open him up?" Dave said. "Can you set me up on a payment plan?" He got up and wandered into the front hall with the cell phone.

I knew the farm had stretched us out, plus Albert's lump removal, and I imagined colic surgery wouldn't be cheap. With a year of debt behind us, we had only recently stopped eating breakfast and lunch for dinner.

Dave hung up with the vet. "They're taking Shorty in now." He sat down in the family room. "Darlene thinks surgery won't work. She's seen things go south on horses Shorty's age." Dave's eyes were fixed in space on no particular place.

"Sixteen for a horse isn't that ancient, is it?" I said.

Dave shrugged but didn't answer.

"It's Shorty Bones," I said. "We have to try." The look on Dave's face and the tilt of his head made me worried for him. I took hold of his arms and held him away from me a little so I could look directly into his face. There was deep sadness in his red, sunken eyes.

"I gave the go-ahead, Renata. We'll see what happens," he said.

"You did the right thing." I wrapped my arms around my husband and pulled him close.

Dave squeezed me tight. "Once he takes a look inside, the vet will have a better idea what we're dealing with."

I was happy we were on the same save-Shorty-Bones page.

Within less than an hour, the cell phone rang again. Dave answered it on speaker. In the background there was an ominous sound. The vet had literally called from the operating room with the horse cut wide open. The deep rhythmic sound was Shorty's sedated breathing.

"It's a blockage, where the small bowel meets the stomach," the vet said.

Dave and I exchanged a glance. He appeared at a loss for words, so I jumped in. "What do you think it is?"

"Looks like worm larva."

"Worms?" I said.

"This is good news," said the vet. "We'll just clear things out, shorten the small bowel slightly and then join it to the stomach."

"Shorty has a chance?" Dave and I both said in unison.

"Yes. Shorty has a good chance. May I go ahead?"

"Definitely," Dave shot back.

Driving up Guelph Line, I stopped at the hospital and visited Shorty a few times after his surgery. The large belly bandage radiated bright white against his dark bay coat. With each encounter, the horse tried to squeeze into my back pocket, nose first. When I opened the stall door to leave for home, it was as if he were hiding behind me and expecting to sneak out with me, unnoticed.

I hardly knew the vet who performed the surgery; we only spoke a few words. Yet we were connected by our love of horses and by my gratitude to him and his team. In vet medicine there's a saying: "Two days, two weeks, two months, two years." If the animal made it to one milestone, then it was more likely to make it to the next.

Shorty Bones made a full recovery. He rejoined his best friend Are You Pan Enough, once more chomping fallen apples in the orchard paddock.

It took us a year to pay off the colic surgery. Albert's leg healed nicely and he moved over to be with the trainer. My thought was that Dave Lumsden was put on this earth to save horses.

But Dave's generosity and patience toward our small Standardbred herd would soon be tested and stretched beyond imagination. It would be many months before we were able to fully comprehend the cost and commitment involved in owning a farm and building a new barn and arena. At the start of the project, it all seemed simple. In the end, travelling up the steep construction path and stick-handling around Mother Nature's challenges in the process became a kind of hard education.

Renata Lumsden

Chapter 13

LIFE AND DEATH IN THE COLD

In Ontario, the winter of 2016 was one of the mildest on record. On February 3 of that same year, Hamilton was Canada's weather hotspot as the thermometer rose to sixteen degrees Celsius. Temperatures were eight degrees higher than the previous high set twenty-five years earlier.

Dave and I enjoyed the break from Old Man Winter but couldn't help but sit back in amazement. Just one year earlier, in 2015, the pregnant mares had been huddled in the frozen fields, the mercury had sunk lower and lower, and snow had engulfed the farm. The new barn and arena build, with all its starts and stops, had continued from January through to April that year.

"I can still feel it sometimes," I said across the restaurant table. A piping hot pizza sat between us. "That cold was beyond bitter."

Dave sprinkled a few chili flakes on his slices. "This winter would have been *so* much easier for the new build."

"And cheaper," I said.

Dave just shook his head.

"But we did it." I grinned. I was still in awe that we had built both a barn and an arena despite last year's crazy cold.

In 2015, Darlene and Derrick had rigged the waterers with power and back-up generators to ensure the life-sustaining liquid never froze. The couple bundled up and ran from paddock to paddock night and day inspecting the horses. Construction pressed on despite conditions that were barely fit for man or beast.

Each morning, with sunrise hardly an hour old, the work crew showed up and put in a full day's performance. We were thankful for their determination and consistent attendance. Workers directed portable heaters at the ground to warm the earth. The artificial heat drove out the frost so the men could pour foundations and move forward with other temperature-sensitive construction to stay on schedule.

Later, roofers swaddled in layers looked like parka balloons with gloved hands as they swung hammers and shifted about against the icy blast. The job-site manager rotated shifts among the skilled trades—from outside to inside—to extend productivity and keep menacing frostbite from delicate fingers, faces, and toes. Despite everyone's best efforts, the bitter cold often slowed things down. Human or horse, everyone, including Dave and I, could only wait patiently for the build to progress.

In the original wood barn, temporary stalls had been set up to maximize space and accommodate the greatest horse numbers. Albert and his young friends spent their nights inside, where collectively they helped provide a source of warmth. Until the new build was completed, there simply wasn't enough stall space for every colt, gelding, filly, and mare at Hillsborough Stables. Pan and Shorty had their spot outside. Lido and the other mares spent nights with their backs turned to the biting winds in minus-forty-degree temperatures. The geldings and mares had not been clipped.

Renata Lumsden

Instead they grew thick winter coats, which insulated them, keeping the warmth next to their skin. With a run-in shed in each paddock, the horses could also seek shelter and stay reasonably dry and comfortable despite the cutting cold.

Queen Lusi was a different case. She'd occupied a stall at the far end of the old barn, away from Albert's gang. In the stall next to Lusi, a mare and her foal enjoyed a reprieve from the bitter cold. As I watched, our mare often adjusted her head height so she could stare through the small gaps between the boards. With her gaze fixed, she had stood quietly, minute after minute, peeking at the mother–baby pair. I wondered if she missed motherhood.

Eventually after that awful winter, the snow stopped and the last door hinge at the farm was hung in place. The swallows found a new rafter or two inside the arena and began constructing their small, cup-shaped mud nests. Bursting bags of fresh stall shavings were cut open and spread inside each stall, like welcome mats in a new horse hotel. Hillsborough Stables was now fully functional.

"Thank goodness that's all behind us now." Dave popped one last bite of pizza crust into his mouth.

His words woke me from my musings. "For sure." I looked down. My plate was still half full.

"Magic's racing this week," Dave said. "I have a late meeting that night."

"I'll go up to support our girl," I told him.

A few days later, I was standing trackside. The night sky held a sliver of a moon. I knew where most people were. Home. Glued to their TVs. Only horse owners and true harness-racing fans would be at Flamboro Downs tonight, I thought, because game seven of the World Series was on. Despite being on the road, the Cubs prevailed in the tenth.

I caught the baseball game only from the seventh inning because Mach Magic was hitting the track around 9:00 p.m.

that night. In southern Ontario, a misty November rain fell throughout the evening. The tote board registered thirteen degrees Celsius. Alone I walked back and forth under a small awning. My footsteps sounded hollow on the asphalt beside the grandstand. In the distance, a cone of light fell near the large exit of the backstretch barn. I stopped a minute to listen for the horses as they made their way onto the race-track. I wanted to call out Magic's name. Instead, I kept my eyes low, looking for her single white hind sock.

A talented field of seven mares paced past me in the post parade. An eighth entry had been scratched. Mach Magic had drawn the four-hole post position. I was grateful for the mild temperatures, although I had to wipe wet sprinkles from my phone camera face. Still, the rain didn't deter my enthusiasm or the urge to take some pictures and a short video clip of our big bay four-year-old for Dave. I brushed my face with my sleeve to clear away the rain and noticed a small crowd milling about. My ears perked up. A handful of other owners had also come out to support their mares. I overheard them. Each one had a story, with hopes resting on a new trainer, driver, or piece of racing equipment.

Scotty Coulter sat in the sulky for us. He used to drive mother Lusi and had driven Magic for the first time the week prior, coming third. The ninth race on tonight's card was also the biggest purse payout. I held my breath when the field took off behind the starter's car. Their hooves beat out a rhythmic symphony against the moist dirt track.

Mach Magic departed sharply. The field pressed on to the first turn. Maxim Seelster drove to the outside and took the lead, but Mach Magic reclaimed the front in the straight-away, while Sports Expert paced away in third. Sauble Ashley moved on the outside at a length and a quarter back from my girl and appeared to be getting closer.

"Mach Magic still has the lead and looks strong," shouted the announcer.

Renata Lumsden

My heart fluttered and I finally remembered to breathe. Running along beside the track barrier, I felt as if my legs, arms, and hands were moving in slow motion. Everything near me seemed to slow down too, with the exception of the charging horses. Mach Magic drove on for home. She hit the wire in a respectable time of 1:56.2 seconds. Tonnes of hurling horseflesh and colourful bikes and drivers raced by me. The entire field crossed the finish line with Mach Magic out in front. She'd won!

Scotty let the horse finish her race by pacing right around the oval track. I appreciated the breather myself as the race result sunk in. The tote board flashed before me. It was Magic's seventh lifetime win. The race finished up with Maxim Seelster in second, Sports Expert in third, and Sauble Ashley in fourth.

As the owners of the first-place horse, we took home just over $4,000. Success was measured in moments, not money, but I knew the extra funds helped. I eventually managed to control my dizzy euphoria and steady myself on the track just as my girl came up to the winner's circle. I called to her.

"Hi, Magic." With head held high, the horse stopped and gave me a stare of acknowledgement through her blinkers before the driver nudged her forward.

"I thought that was you," Scotty said, his face wet and muddy.

It had been years since I'd spoken to him, yet his bright eyes still shone with youthfulness. It took a second for me to find my tongue. "Great drive. She came home strong, like her mommy." I smiled and hoped he hadn't noticed my lip quiver.

Meanwhile, Chantal Mitchell, our new trainer for Magic for the past seven months, zoomed up from the backstretch barn in a golf cart and jumped out. The horse seemed to respond a little better to women, and we'd been looking for a change of luck for our mare. Chantal's broad smile took over her face and almost swallowed up her eyes. We gave each other a hug and then scattered, taking our positions beside the horse.

I stood proudly in the winner's circle and the flash went off. But on the walk back to the grandstand, I found myself thinking of how a combination of chance and tragedy earlier in 2016 had brought Chantal together with Mach Magic, Dave, and me.

In the late evening hours of January 4, the small community of Puslinch, Ontario, slept while fire ripped through a barn at a training facility called Classy Lane Stables. Sharp, biting winter cold couldn't dull the flames or aid the helpless victims. The structure on fire, known as Barn 1, contained more than forty horses. The story hit the local papers and online horse-related agencies fast. I remembered reading the news that morning and feeling torn—torn between immense sadness for those affected, especially the horses, and gratitude that none of ours were involved.

Chantal Mitchell and her boyfriend and fellow trainer, Kris DiCenzo, discovered the blaze on their way back, with a single horse in tow, from racing at Woodbine Racetrack. It was the worst time of day and the worst season for a fire. While the towering red inferno shot up into the cold, black night sky, Chantal and Kris, an army of two, stood by help-lessly. The flames engulfed the wood-and-steel structure so fast that they weren't able to get to the horses. The couple watched in horror as their life and extended equine family burned on. The firefighters arrived, their hoses choked with ice at times, but they managed to stop the licking heat from spreading to a handful of nearby stables filled with just as many more harness-racing horses. Only Chantal's horse—a four-year-old bay named Rakin It In—and another trainer's six-year-old, who was also racing that night, had avoided the fiery fist of death.

The rising sun the next morning only confirmed the grim reality, and clean-up began. Workers used heavy equipment to discreetly and respectfully cover the charred remains with straw. Horse people gathered; the barn contained both their livelihood and their loved ones. Horse racing was more than just a business here—it was a way of life for the people of Puslinch and the surrounding community. The death of over forty horses left owners, trainers, and grooms to deal with the dramatic loss. At least twenty people at the heart of the tragedy were out of work. A stable could be restocked and the necessary gear and items replaced. But it was impossible to replace the Standardbred personalities lost in the fire.

Overnight, freshly painted barnboard plaques adorned thick trunks of mature trees. Makeshift gravestones, they lined the long driveway leading into Classy Lane Stables, where they remained for weeks. One of Albert's mates from Hillsborough, another two-year-old, Stretch Run, perished in the blaze. His name stood out as we drove by. A handful of horses, from two-year-olds that had yet to race to six-year-old geldings, had recently returned to Barn 1 from turnout time off at Hillsborough Stables, only to meet their untimely demise.

The swell of an online fundraiser through GoFundMe attempted to raise $100,000 in an effort to help. Thanks to social media, word spread. Animal and horse lovers everywhere united. In the end, the fund amassed more than six times the intended target.

With clean-up behind them, trainers, grooms, and owners moved forward and began the process of rebuilding. A large temporary fabric structure at Classy Lane allowed those most affected to start anew with horses and resume training.

Meanwhile, a brand new wood-and-steel configuration called Barn 6 was erected on the property and opened in

May. By this time, Mach Magic had been training under Chantal for nearly five months. Behind the new barn in the centre of a turnabout stood a memorial to the fire. The first time I saw it, I froze. Dave and I pulled in and parked. He ran inside to chat with Chantal and see Magic, but the memorial called to me. Maybe it was my strict Catholic upbringing, but I'd always felt drawn to graves.

A circular rim of brick pavers had been assembled around a young oak tree. For strength? For vitality? To proclaim life? Or to mark death? I wondered if that hardy species with its lobed, deciduous leaves was chosen for all those reasons. The circle of paving stones reminded me of the racetrack and the cycle of life, I found myself pondering death and rebirth.

Flanking the oak, two sandy-grey rectangular headstones bore the horses' names. My breath caught in my throat at the sight of that long list. Losing a horse must be like losing a child, I thought; no one really recovers. The names of those who perished were etched in black against the cold granite. Nearby, two chunky stone benches allowed visitors like me to respectfully sit. The surface of one stone bench was etched with the silhouette of a harness racehorse in full stride, pulling a faceless driver on a sturdy bike. Above the horse were the words "In Memory of the Beloved Horses of Barn 1."

The modest height of each tombstone surprised me at first until I started reading: one stone contained names starting with letters *A* to *M*, and the other finished the list. The names of three miniature horses—Daisy, her baby Margarita, and little gelding Sammy—were carved together on the final line, and a cat named BG was also included. That day, I wiped away the tears as I read.

Among all the harness-racing sadness and loss earlier in the year, Magic's win at Flamboro Downs and the story about Lusi the champion Standardbred and Albert her preemie foal were there for us when there wasn't a lot of happy horse news to smile about.

By chance and perhaps some irony, Mach Magic had ended up at Classy Lane Stables. Dave had moved her over from Ted's to Chantal's barn a month after the fire.

We were reassured by the fact that Classy Lane's owners had now added state-of-the-art fire-prevention technology and protocols. As the facility's name suggested, it was highly regarded before the fire. Now, with the addition of heat and smoke detectors, timed dryers, surge protectors (the cause of the fire had been determined to be electrical), and other fire safety measures, Classy Lane was now one of the safest facilities around.

Horses didn't jump from trainer to trainer on a regular basis; at least ours didn't. The trainer–horse–groom relationship took time to evolve. Mach Magic had moved over to Ted from Travis and had been under Ted's care as a two- and three-year-old. She'd done well, coming "in the money" in nearly 60 percent of her racing starts. But changing trainers allowed fresh eyes on the horse and a new approach for realizing the animal's racing potential. And the groundswell to help those involved after the fire fit in with our timeline to change things up in the trainer department with Mach Magic.

"I'm so sorry for your loss," I said—we both said—to Chantal when we first met her and Kris. We said it because we meant it, but the words couldn't match the seismic vibration of the collective grief experienced by those affected. The miniature horses had belonged to her and her groom, and she and Kris had been training several of the horses who'd died.

I tried not to dwell on the fire and past lives lost. I believed in time's power to heal. I saw a promising present day for Mach Magic and I wished for a bright harness-racing future for Magical Albert too. However, it wasn't at all clear if Albert would cooperate with Ted and make it to the track.

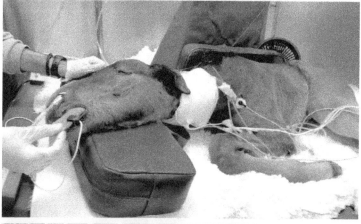

　　　　　　　Renata Lumsden

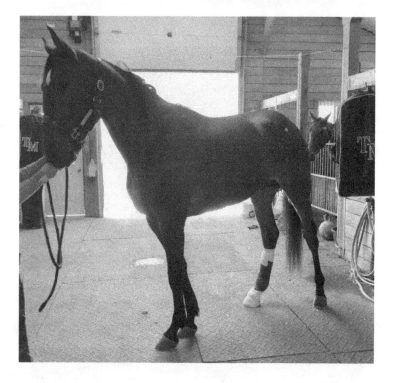

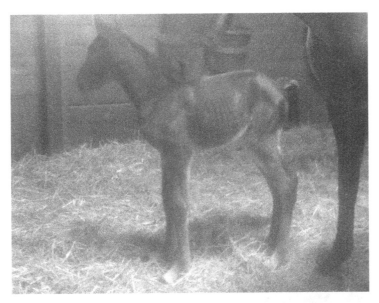

Magical Albert

Renata Lumsden

Magical Albert

Chapter 14

BALLS AND BABIES

While Mach Magic had been busy with Chantal garnering wins at the track, Albert had been busy too—kicking. Our boy was known to kick. Kick through stall walls. Kick at grooms. Kick up at stall windows. In fact, he'd once managed to catch a hind foot in a window. Luckily, Shawna hadn't been too far off. She heard Albert's frantic whinny before she noticed he was hung up. It took two grooms to free him. Albert's behaviour had led to some interior decorating at Ted's place that involved thick rubber mats halfway up the stall walls and crosshatched bars on the windows. I wish I could say the changes were common among smart, talented harness racehorses, but no other stall in Ted's barn resembled Albert's.

Since birth, Albert had always done things his way and in his time. I shrugged off his exuberant behaviour as the result of his preemie status, but others were getting concerned. Albert, now two years and nine months old, was big and strapping, and he might do some serious damage if he continued to develop his kicking skills.

"Renata," Dave said to me one night, "Ted says we have to consider gelding him."

"But he's Lusi's only son—we may be losing an important potential sire if we do!"

I recoiled from the idea of having my big handsome boy castrated, even though the majority of colts underwent the procedure. Intact stallions could be a handful, their minds more on mating than racing. And they often needed special stabling and turnout arrangements to keep them from hopping fences to breed mares or fight with geldings. Still, I argued in Albert's favour, trying to buy time until he eventually settled down.

Albert's sisters had never gone under the knife. They were as perfect today as the day they entered the world. In my mind, horses, female or male, were born into pure perfection. The way they entered the world was the way they should leave it, unless the situation turned into a question of life and death.

My ectopic pregnancy had definitely fit into the life-and-death category. If Dave hadn't nudged me along to go to the hospital, I don't know that I'd still be here. I knew I wasn't feeling well, but I thought that it would eventually pass while I sat around for the following eight months until the baby was due. "Don't touch what isn't broken" was how I felt about health and wellness, and life in general.

The birth of Lusi's only son—our first colt—shocked and surprised me even though I knew the gender odds were equal. His survival struck me as a blessing. Surely Albert was meant for something? After all the medical intervention he went through so early, it felt unfair now to put him through more, and in so doing cut off Lusi's and Albert's bloodline by gelding him. It seemed very clear to me: Albert just needed time, and eventually things would be fine.

Besides, this was an elective surgery we were talking about. As a healthcare worker, I knew all too well that any surgical procedure using anaesthesia ran the risk of complications, even though the risk was low in this situation. Still, was it worth taking in Albert's case? For me, the one who didn't see Albert every day or work with him, surgery appeared totally unnecessary. Castrating a healthy specimen like Albert made me think of sterilization. No thanks. Turning a perfectly fertile creature into a eunuch carried outdated overtones from the Dark Ages for me.

Unfortunately, the added weeks of my energetic protest against gelding didn't yield much improvement in Albert. Eventually, I had to succumb. Albert was gelded in mid-October and sent to Hillsborough to recuperate.

In early February 2017, I had a day off. I set out just before 10:00 a.m. to visit the horses. The excitement I felt inside kept me warm on my journey through farm country. By the time I arrived in Moffat, the temperature had dropped significantly. It didn't matter.

My first stop was a nearby tack shop for new halters for Lusi, Lido, and Albert. I was also on the lookout for a new indoor horse toy. Albert had mashed and beaten up his last one. He invariably turned giant-size Jolly Balls into a shredded mess of rubber after only a few months. I'd never seen a horse play with one until Albert came along.

"Play" wasn't really the right word because Albert bashed, smashed, and tossed the ball with all the force he could muster while stall-bound. During a late morning visit to Ted's barn six months earlier—perhaps at the height of Albert's boredom that day—he'd treated me to a show. The ball was always loose on the floor, partly covered with shavings, in one corner or another of his stall. Without warning, Albert grabbed the big ball handle in his mouth and pounded the ball into the nearest stall wall. He kept thrusting his entire body up against the wall until he appeared to rock back and forth, while the wall did the same dance. For the finale, Albert bobbed up and down with the ball handle in his mouth and finally released the toy high up over the rafters, after which it landed beside the horse in the stall next door. If I'd been sitting, I'd have leapt up to give Albert a standing ovation.

Derrick had given me specific instructions for the ball purchases: "No red ones this time." I wondered if he simply didn't like the colour red, or if there was some superstition at play. When I pressed him further about the colour, he said, "Horses don't see red, but they can see blues and greens." I knew Albert wasn't partial. Along the back wall of the store I counted one, two, three Jolly Balls in red. Lower down, I noticed two more in chartreuse. I let out a faint laugh; they were coming home with me.

By the time I turned onto Campbellville Road, the snow had started falling. A multitude of tiny flakes soon became a shaken snow globe. I slowed down a few times, but my tires felt like they were hugging the road. So despite the weather, I stopped to pick up coffee and butter tarts at Dar's Delights.

"What have you got there?" Derrick said when I walked into the barn, my arms full. He set his rake down and ran over.

"Coffee and treats." I set the pastries on a nearby stool.

Derrick grabbed the coffees. "You didn't have to do that."

Darlene came around the corner, a grim look on her face. "We're really behind today," she said. "One of my stable girls swerved to avoid a deer on the way to work. She's at the hospital."

"Oh my gosh!" I pressed a coffee into her hand. "How is she?"

"She'll be fine, but the car's a write-off." Darlene tugged her toque snug to her head with her free hand.

"I'm glad she's okay. Here," I said, offering Darlene a tart, "I'll be right back."

I must have looked like one of Santa's helpers when I returned from the car carrying two big green Jolly Balls and a tote full of halters.

"Who gets the balls again?" Derrick asked.

"Albert for sure," I said. "I'm heading up to Ted's farm next."

"Ted texted early this morning," Darlene said. "Albert settled in nicely. And he's fully healed from the gelding procedure." She took another sip of coffee.

I could feel myself getting choked up. "I still can't believe we had him gelded."

"That horse kicked holes in two stalls while he was here," Darlene said, shaking her head.

I was about to take a big bite of butter tart, but this stopped me. "Really? I thought castrating a horse was supposed to calm him?"

"It takes time for male hormones to die down," Darlene said. "Trust me, it was the right thing to do. And gelding him will also help Albert fill out. He'll get stronger in the hind end."

"Yeah, I guess." I was relieved she didn't go on about the stalls and resent Albert for the damage. Albert could be a bit of a discipline problem at times, but he was *my* discipline problem. I didn't want Darlene or anyone else to think negatively of the horse.

"Albert put weight on while he was here," Derrick added.

"That's good," I finally said, knowing there was no turning back time regarding the stall damage or the gelding procedure.

"Not sure who gets the second Jolly Ball," I said, happy to change the subject. "Maybe Pan and Shorty could share one?"

"No. Not the boys." Darlene wrinkled her nose. "Those boys like to race each other around the paddock. They self-exercise. In between, they patrol the fence line near the entrance and watch out for visitors. I can't see them playing with a ball."

"Maybe Lusi?" I heard my voice rise unnaturally at the prospect of giving my girl the toy. My confidence regarding Lusi's likes and dislikes had never been strong, like a mother who wasn't certain about buying gifts for an older teen. The added vocal volume was meant to support the new idea.

"Not Lusi," Darlene shot back. "That diva won't play with it."

"You don't think so?" I said. It was looking like Albert was going to end up with *two* new balls, which I thought, chuckling to myself, was only fitting, given he'd just lost both of his.

"Gotta run. Thanks for the coffee." Darlene disappeared and Derrick got down to work mucking stalls.

I ran off to see Lusi. Her new stall was much more up front and centre, befitting of the Queen, I thought. She ignored me at first and then poked her head out with ears pinned.

"That's my girl." I let her sniff my hand. "You want your treat?" I'd loaded up with eight boxes of peanut butter bars. Today the snacks would be spread around at Hillsborough, and then I'd take three boxes to Ted's farm for Albert. Lusi offered me a little more attention when I ripped open the wrapper. Her nostrils flared as the peanutty fragrance rose between us. Soon her tongue was flapping and she had crumbs on her chin.

I left my Lusi and burst through the barn doors, headed for the broodmares' paddock. Lido came when I called her name, half waddling, half walking from the run-in shed. A handful of other pregnant mares were already greeting me at the fence. I gave all the ladies carrot slices, but Lido Magic got the most. The fluffiness of her winter coat only added to her size. She looked like a Hummer with legs, not the H2 SUV type, but solid army-grade vehicle complete with chopper clip. The baby was due in less than a week.

From there I ran up the hill to see the boys. Pan was munching hay, while Shorty stood off in a corner doing his business. Pan wandered over and I rewarded him with a packet of bars and a few kisses. Then I meandered down the drive and met up with Shorty. He had barely got through his treat when Pan was upon us. I opened another packet and split it between them just to keep up good manners and to remind the boys how to share.

A short drive up First Line and I hit Ted's place. Driving through the open iron gate, I noticed the row of short, squat pines planted beside the barn, their branches bedecked with snow, and admired the wintry scene.

"Caffeine, anyone?" I said. I closed the barn door to keep out the winter chill, and then added, "Here's some toys for Albert when he's up to having playtime."

"Thanks," Shawna and Ted said in unison.

I pointed. "That java will need a good shot in the microwave."

Albert thrust his head out at the sound of my voice. From the far stall at the end of the shedrow, the horse's deep brown eyes gleamed in the bright barn lighting. Albert's cheek resembled a five-pin bowling ball. I felt the urge to run to him and plant a big wet kiss there.

"How's my boy?" I said.

"Albert's doing great," Ted said. "He starts back training again tomorrow."

I smiled politely, still feeling sad that he'd been gelded. Some hugs and time with Albert swept away the bad. I noticed a new layer of fat and muscle over the horse's ribs and hips. I tried to take comfort in the fact that few males stayed in their stallion form throughout their lives.

I reached up and stroked Albert's forelock. Again and again I whispered, "It's okay." The way he hung his big head over my shoulder and allowed me to speak into his ear gave me the first good feeling I'd had since his surgery. Of course his tongue was sticking out.

If Albert wasn't going to be able to pass on Lusi's genes, then at least her daughter Lido would. Back home in Ancaster, Dave and I were hunkered down in the basement while the cold evening wind howled outside. The floor heating was cranked; one cat had found my lap, the other a nearby chair. A Sunday night of Netflix seemed like a fitting end to the weekend. At 10:45 p.m., just as the movie ended, Dave got a text from Darlene.

"Listen to this," he said, then read aloud: "Lido rubbed her bum against the stall wall. Her water broke and in no time the baby came."

"Lido had the baby!" I jumped up. The cat flew off my lap.

Darlene told us that she and Derrick had stood nearby at the ready.

As soon as Lido's water broke, she folded herself into a knee-deep bed of straw and groaned. Darlene and Derrick moved to help. Another groaning sound, no doubt the result of a contraction, echoed through the barn, followed by the appearance of a small hoof. The foal's second hoof quickly popped out behind the first. Nature's hand at work, a black wet nose shot through next. Derrick and Darlene were right there. The baby slid out. It was a filly.

No red-bag delivery this time—just a nice, straightforward birth, I thought.

"Darlene says she's a good weight at a hundred and fifteen pounds." Dave took me into his arms.

"I can't believe the baby came so fast. Between the snow and the distance, we'd never have made it," I said. Dave was quiet. "What are you thinking?"

"Tomorrow, February thirteenth, is my mother's birthday," he said, his eyes moist. "Maybe it's a sign."

I grabbed his hand, knowing that Dave's first experience with death had come in 2003 with Kathy, his mom; she had become ill unexpectedly and died in hospital from a brain bleed. Some nine years later, Dave's dad, Tom, was diagnosed with terminal cancer. That left Dave, an only child, alone.

The horses and those connected to the sport seemed like an important extended family to Dave. The veil had lifted for me where family was concerned. Now I was beginning to realize that it had lifted for Dave too. His deep connection to the horses told me that I wasn't the only one in this marriage who saw Albert, Lusi, and the others as more than just large pets. Because Dave had no siblings, it made sense to me. Dave had more friends than anyone else I knew, from every realm and facet of his life. He had many close friends too. By instinct, he seemed to put himself in others' shoes, rarely judging but always seeing the good in those he met. In my opinion, he possessed a rare combination of thoughtfulness and loyalty. That loyalty had seeped into his relationship with the horses. The cats and I now ranked just above the herd in importance. I wiped his tears with my hand and kissed his cheek.

We plunked back down on the sofa, his arm around my shoulder, my hair brushing his cheek. Dave's cell phone sat cradled between us. Darlene sent three photos.

The first one showed the spacious broodmare stall, where on a heaping bed of golden straw lay the little filly. Her newborn eyes were open and her muscled body glistened.

"She's a beauty," Dave said, with a quiet smile.

In my eyes the baby's nose and muzzle looked as if Mother Nature had recently dipped both into talcum powder. Right away I noticed something else.

"Look." I pointed. My finger against the screen accidently hid the foal's face. I'd half expected the baby to look like all our other newborns. The excitement of a new foal filled me, but my delight turned to surprise, however, when I noticed something was missing.

"What?" Dave said. He brushed my hand away to examine the image more closely.

"Take your time," I said, hoping the oddity might jump out at Dave.

Dave gave me a confused look and remained silent for a second or two.

"She's missing a star," I finally said. She was a bay, like Lido, but without markings. The similar colouring of the pair in the dim stall lighting made it hard to see where mother stopped and baby started. The beauty of the image struck me, like a painting of an all-black cat against the night sky. Perhaps, I thought, a starless face showed influence from her sire? This foal was different from all our others.

"Look! She made it upright," I said. In two additional images the filly stood. "She's kissing Derrick." I laughed out loud. Derrick had knelt down with his hands on the baby's wide chest. With pointy ears and fuzzy mane and tail, the foal looked anatomically perfect from top to bottom. "Don't you just love her?" I refocused my eyes.

Lido's tongue could be seen behind the foal's right leg, near the baby's rump, still in the process of licking and cleaning her. It looked as though the mare was tolerating the midwives and the photographic moment.

By the time Dave and I finally stopped texting and emailing friends and family to announce the newest arrival in our lives, it was well past midnight. I couldn't stop shaking my head about missing the actual birthing event—Lido's first baby since 2014. I made a note to self: next time I'll need to camp out at the farm.

The following day, after classes and meetings were done at work, I took to Twitter and asked followers to offer a name. With He's Watching as sire and Lido Magic as dam, the filly needed a race name and a barn name. "She's Magic" soon emerged as the winner, with Sheshe as the youngster's barn name. Dave approved and so did Darlene and Derrick.

She's Magic led the Hillsborough Stables foal parade in 2017. I researched the filly's barn name on Google and was surprised at what came up to describe our bundle of energy: On a website called Seven Reflections, I read that the name Sheshe means "You are spiritually intense and can sting or charm. Your name brings love and new starts into life and attracts money. In business, you… enjoy considerable financial success. You have an eventful, exciting life. You are versatile and have the ability to learn easily. You are always looking for a chance to do your own thing, to be your own person, and to have things done your own way."

The last bit about doing things your own way was definitely all Lido. Versatility and an ability to learn would stack the odds in the filly's favour—if indeed she possessed these attributes. But that was that: everyone started to call our new family member Sheshe.

This filly represented a healing salve for our lesions of grief. Dave and I had waited years for Lido to foal out successfully, for Lusi to become a "grandmare." The tragic loss of Lido's firstborn, Sarasota Magic, had thrown us all into a sad state. That little foal would never be forgotten, but the dawn of bright new beginnings eased our sense of loss. Now Lusi's progeny and our herd family were expanding, and with them, in Sheshe's case, the hope that another smart, talented champion might bloom from within the bunch. Sheshe was still years away from racing—if she did make it. But Dave and I were already sure she had it in her.

Chapter 15

MORE BONES TO PICK

Unusual summery spells during January and February 2017 saw temperatures climb well into the high teens, and they were still the closest thing to warm temperatures by mid-May that same year. A cool spring captured nature's colours a little longer, and the forsythia and daffodils held their bright yellow hue for what seemed like months.

It was May 10. A regular Wednesday by most accounts, except where Albert was concerned.

Dave worked a full day and was planning to join more than two dozen folks later at a restaurant in town. My husband was helping lead a fundraising dinner for the new hybrid operating unit at the local heart hospital. I'd just arrived in Toronto after work when my phone rang. I had a hunch it was about Albert.

A gelded Albert had been back training with Ted for several months and had recently posted a 2:10 seconds mile at Mohawk Raceway. Despite the progress, my intuition told me something wasn't quite right. Albert had gone off his granola treats. The horse had taken to biting me and pinning back his ears. Also, I'd noticed Albert move away in the wash stall when the water blast hit his right ankle.

I'd been going through some personal age-related changes lately and didn't want to overreact. Long nights of hot, sweaty, interrupted sleep were offset by a balanced diet, sunshine in small doses, and fitness prescribed by Dr. Me, but still I couldn't shake the feeling about Albert in the pit of my stomach.

After work one night, I followed Dave into the family room and wondered why I felt so sensitive, as though if he said anything at all, I'd burst out crying—I who had hardly cried in the past. We sat together on the sofa.

Through tears that came from nowhere, the words tumbled out of my mouth. "Something's wrong," I said.

"What?" Dave leaned in toward me.

"I just know it." I tried not to blubber too noisily.

"With Albert?"

"Yes." I coughed the word out between sobs, unable to control the emotions.

"He's fine, Renata," Dave said, his gaze sensitive. He reached out and rubbed my back.

"Something's changed," I squeaked in a tiny, tense voice.

"Changed?" Dave said. "How?"

"I want Albert to have a full physical in Guelph," I blurted.

"Guelph?" Dave's head shot back. "Why Guelph?"

"Albert started there. They know him." I stopped to wipe my eyes and nose with my sleeve. "Our boy needs X-rays and a work-up."

"Okay. Okay." Dave gave me a reassuring smile.

"He's a special horse." The sobs took over. My shoulders trembled between gasps of air.

"Leave it with me." Dave reached for my hand.

"Fresh eyes on Albert won't hurt," I said, regaining my composure.

"Okay."

Now, sitting in a downtown Toronto lobby, I rifled through my purse. AC/DC's "Run Away Train" ringtone blasted from inside it. I fumbled for the phone and Dave's name flashed before me. "Hi, love," I said.

Dave had recently consulted Travis and Ted about my concerns with Albert. The young trainer turned ready-mix truck driver and our current trainer for Albert had both offered Dr. Ruch as a solution. Dave knew that the old-timer vet in Barrie, Ontario, had a history of diagnosing equine problems both while stationary and while sitting behind the animal in the jog cart on the track. I'd agreed to let the savvy eyes of Dr. Ruch on Albert, instead of those in Guelph.

"Where are you?" Dave said.

"In Toronto for a meeting," I replied.

"Ted took Albert up to see Dr. Ruch today."

I steeled myself. "What's the news?"

"Well. Albert's got a few issues," Dave said.

"And?" My mind took off racing through a list of possible findings, one more ominous than the next.

"First of all," Dave said, "the vet isn't concerned about the extra bones in Albert's legs."

"The calcinosis circumscripta?" I said. "Are you sure the vet saw it all?"

"Ruch took X-rays. Albert's fine with those extra bones where they are."

In my mind in the past, I'd seen a debilitated older Albert with sad eyes and bony sacks sticking out all over his legs. I wiped away the old images. "What else did the vet say?"

"Albert's got a few shin splints," Dave said.

I stood up. "What's that again?"

"All race horses get those from training, like runners, so—"

"Is that it?" I interrupted.

"There's an issue with the ankle."

"Which one?"

"The right one."

"I knew it." This time my own voice echoed in my head.

"You were right," Dave said.

"I *knew* it. When he——"

"Let me finish."

"Okay. Sorry." I sat down in the hopes it would help temper my agitation.

"There's bone chips and they need to come out." Dave paused. "Remove those, and Albert will be fine."

I stopped to think, imagining small white fragments of bone in a horse's ankle.

"He's not limping, but they're bothering him when he races. It's not great news, but it's an easy fix," Dave said. "Timelines to make it to racing might get screwed up, but that's kind of the way it is."

It definitely was kind of the way it always was with Albert, I thought. No one was exactly sure how or why Albert's back ankle had developed an issue. But it was the same ankle he'd caught up in the stall window a few years earlier. The same ankle the horse had busted through two stalls once during time off for the gelding procedure. But when or where or how, it wasn't important now.

I knew that not all Standardbred racehorses had it in them to make it to the track. Those athletes that did have it in them often made their debut on the one-mile oval as two- or three-year-olds. In the midst of his three-year-old season, Albert was headed for surgery. Again. However, the vet told Dave he'd seen horses sour on racing with this type of issue, but it always turned out for the best after surgery for a well-bred and well-put-together big horse like Albert.

On a sunny Thursday in May, the horse trailer pulled up to Milton Equine Hospital on Guelph Line. Albert would stay overnight and go under the knife the following day.

I tried not to fret, but this was Albert's third surgery since birth, and his second within the past eight months—at least two more surgeries than most colts. But Albert always seemed to find a way to steer away from the norm.

Dave walked in from work the next day and dropped his sunglasses and keys on the shelf. "The vet called. Albert's surgery went well," he said.

"Thank goodness!" I exhaled a long sigh of relief. "When can he go home?"

"In a few days," Dave said.

"I hope they send some calming medication with Albert."

Dave looked sideways. "What do you mean?"

"Albert's the world's greatest stall kicker. He'll need stall rest, not confined kicking time."

Dave smiled and waved a hand in my direction. "He'll be fine."

Two days later, on the Saturday of the Victoria Day long weekend, a repaired Albert went back to Ted's barn. Looking a little confused at the tape sock on his ankle, Albert stood still with ears pricked and head turned as if he were listening to us talk about his health and well-being. Ted would take care of him while our gelding recovered, then Albert would leave Ted's farm. The trainer had been holding Albert's reins for nearly two years, but as with Mach Magic the previous year, the time had come for a change. There were no bad feelings on either side. Anthony Beaton had enthusiastically agreed to become Magical Albert's new trainer, and Albert's stall in Barn 4 was all prepared and waiting for him at Classy Lane Stables.

Renata Lumsden

I felt glad that Albert's latest surgery was behind him. Later that evening, Dave and I talked about Albert's journey up to this point.

"It was never meant to be easy for our boy," my husband said with a quick smile. "He'll make it to the big leagues and race in his own good time."

Dave and I were sharing the comfy sectional, and both cats had joined the family discussion. Their silent presence, with Joy across my lap and Martha on her chair beside Dave, completed our circle.

"I hope Albert makes it." I gave Joy a long pat as I spoke. Her eyes closed slowly. In my dreams, I'd vividly seen Albert racing. I hoped my dreams wouldn't be too far off the mark as far as reality was concerned.

"Don't give up on Albert," Dave said. "He does it his way."

At last I understood what was working its way through Dave and me: we desired, despite every hurdle in the path, to help a struggling Albert, in the same way one might provide extra care and support to a much-loved family member. And I saw then that as horse owners, something in us had shifted.

Dave and I weren't newcomers to harness racing. Over the years, we'd owned (in part or in entirety), cheered for, and supported dozens of Standardbreds. We'd also seen dozens leave us and move on to other owners and trainers— I cried for a week the first time we had to let a horse go after a claiming race. Being involved in the harness-racing business meant horses moved around from barn to barn and owner to owner. For us, the emotional attachment was always there, but it was different back then. Lusi and her babies, though, had changed our perspective. The need was stronger in us now: to stand by Albert and offer him every possible chance to succeed as a racehorse. It made sense to me; good people didn't abandon family members in need, they just kept finding new ways to encourage and support them.

I smiled and said a silent prayer.

Chapter 16

TRACKING THE HERD

Meanwhile, the unpredictability of the sport and of the horses involved continued to rear its head. Albert's ankle surgery meant that our young gelding was sidelined at the height of his third year. In 2017, harness racing was caught up in a wave of sweeping changes, including a multi-million-dollar investment to bring year-round racing to Mohawk Racetrack and allow Woodbine to focus on the Thoroughbred arm of the sport. That meant that if Albert made it to the Standardbred big leagues, he'd eventually take a turn on the A-track in Milton.

With trainer Ted MacDonnell, Albert had become acquainted with the job of being a racehorse—right from lining up behind the starting gate while pulling the jog cart to hours of training miles logged. For almost two years, Ted and his grooms had cared for and brought Albert along. On August 1, 2017, Tony Beaton officially became Albert's new trainer.

Born in Cape Breton, Tony was in his late thirties. T-shirts, mainly white, and worn black jeans were the horseman's "go to" in the barn, along with a silver-and-black ball cap—embroidered with "Anthony Beaton Stables"—that sat atop tightly cropped, jet-black hair. Slight of build, he also sported a lopsided smile revealing sparkling teeth. Tony worked with his wife, Lisa, and his groom, Nadine: not exactly an entourage, but both female members of his racing team had been around harness racing for decades, and they loved horses and the sport.

On moving day, the burning August sun had reached its highest point when Tony pulled into Ted's facility with an empty horse trailer in tow. Tony told us that he smiled when he laid eyes on Albert. The youngster's massive size filled the stall; his hind end reached high into the air, and his dark eyes shone above the horizontal line of grey hairs that cut across the middle of his nose. Without any fuss, Albert stepped onto the trailer and into a new chapter of his life.

The next August morning, warm, thick rays of sunshine danced across our kitchen floor. The date marked a special anniversary for us. Sitting at the kitchen table, I felt conflicted in my thoughts and emotions.

"I can't believe he's been gone for eight years."

Dave filled his cereal bowl and joined me. "I know."

We missed Clint, the best man at our wedding, throughout the year, but particularly each August. Like a brother from another mother, Clint may not have been related to Dave by blood, but because they'd grown up together, he was the closest thing to a sibling Dave ever had. Pancreatic cancer took our friend too early at the age of forty-five. I skimmed through Facebook posts about Clint—my husband had intentionally managed to steer clear of social media his entire life—and so I peppered Dave with information about the comments and pictures that were cropping up to commemorate the eight-year anniversary of Clint's death.

My busy fingers quickly added our heartfelt message to the growing number of condolences. I looked up and noticed Dave's milk-covered lip quiver, so I changed the subject.

"Today marks a new start for Albert." I smiled and Dave half smiled back. Picking up my bowl and juice glass, I sauntered to the sink. "Any news yet from Tony?"

As if to illustrate the trainer's promise to keep us posted, an image of Albert basking in early morning sunbeams came up on Dave's phone. The horse's bay coat glowed, giving definition to the bulging muscles of his chest and legs. His long, lustrous tail sailed sideways behind him as if disconnected. Despite the tiny, two-dimensional image, I could practically feel the strength surging from Albert's powerful neck. The horse's head was tilted and half in shadow. Even so, his eyes were bright. The contrast of light and dark across his face allowed the veining to stand out beneath his irregular star. The photo's caption read,

He's a big boy.

Remembrances of and sadness about Clint surrounded us, yet at the same time we were excited about a fresh beginning for our youngster. It was no wonder that Tony marvelled at the three-year-old's size, I thought. A big boy for sure at 16.1 hands, Albert wasn't finished growing or filling out.

That same August, Mach Magic notched another career win. Her earnings now sat just below the $100,000 mark. Our mare had unknowingly helped carry us over the debt mountain to a much more level financial ground. The horses, the farm, the debt, everything seemed to settle into a calm, even keel.

And then Dave's phone rang. We were driving home from a coffee shop when the call came through. He answered it on the hands-free.

"Hey, Dave." It was Darlene. "We have a problem here." She sounded rushed.

Dave looked at me across the front seat. "What's up?"

"There's no water at the house," Darlene said.

Dave gripped the steering wheel tighter. "The barn still has water? Have you checked the well?"

Yep. The barn's fine. The well's fine," Darlene said. "Something's wrong between the well and the house. I called a company. They'll be here within the hour."

Dave turned up our driveway. "At least it's early. Lots of daylight to figure it out."

"The company promises a same-day remedy. I'll let you know."

Darlene sent Dave text messages and pictures throughout the afternoon and into the early evening hours. A small trench was dug midway between the well and house to locate the clog. New pipe replaced the stopped-up older piece, and a new pump inside the house finished off the repair. A combination of time and materials saw the bill balloon significantly, although a decent warranty was also included. The call from the repairman finally came as we finished cleaning up after a late dinner, and I heard Dave rhyme off the Visa number just before Mach Magic went to post.

Mach Magic, now aged five, had developed a reputation for serious speed off the starter's gate. Flying forward, she usually landed in the top three along the rail and could manoeuvre gracefully around the turns like her mother. But Magic's initial finishing speed—fourth quarter fraction— had started disappearing. Dave and I, and especially Dave, had wondered whether or not the time had come to start Mach Magic on the broodmare path, like her mother Lusi and sister Lido.

We discussed Magic's development and her training from age three to the present. In the end, rather than send her to the broodmare pasture, we'd changed up her training regime one more time in January of 2017. Magic stayed put at Classy Lane, but she moved over from Chantal in Barn 6 to Tony Beaton's facility in Barn 4. With both Mach Magic and Magical Albert under Tony's care, our equine–trainer relationship now formed a perfect circle. He had all our racehorses, even if there were only two.

"I'm glad we gave Magic another shot at racing," Dave said. He moved closer to me on the basement sectional.

"She's been racing well with Tony." I fumbled with my phone, and the feed on my cell finally picked up Western Fair racetrack in London, Ontario, just as the clock struck midnight. I clicked on race replays.

The skies opened up on the video and let out a deluge of rain during the pre-race post parade. Hearing Dave's name mentioned as breeder and owner, along with our homebred Mach Magic, never got old. The video panned the field of horses and showed some amazing close-ups, both of the animals and the grounds. The green grass of the oval infield shimmered like diamonds thanks to the track lighting that reflected off an army of tiny rain droplets. Nearby trees bulged with freshly sprouted buds. Meanwhile, our horse strutted by all big and strong, with one shiny wet white sock.

Against a field of eight well-qualified mares, Mach Magic took off from the four-hole with Robert Shepherd sitting in the sulky. Robert came from a horse family; he was originally from out east like Tony, and they were good friends. Soft-spoken, with great hands in the bike, he had a steady, honest way about him. Dave and I sat back and watched as the starter's car moved away from the wall of oncoming horseflesh. Its gates retracted like the wings of a giant metal bird, then the vehicle flew off to the side. The sound of pounding hoofbeats rose in crescendo. They were off.

Magic and Robert seemed to almost slingshot off the first turn to take the lead. The group of glistening mares sped along as if they were moving through a community car wash. Fat drops of sideways rain pelted everything as the competitors drove on.

Knowing the outcome of the race in advance made it so much easier on my eyes and my stomach. I couldn't push "replay" enough times. That burst of power, and the slight shaking of her head side to side as her strides increased—Magic reminded me so much of her mother.

With the kick of his left foot at the three-quarter pole, Robert popped her ear plugs. I knew the two small pieces of racing equipment helped the horse concentrate by blocking out certain sounds. Releasing the ear plugs occurred with the kick of a string that connected the plugs and the driver's foot. The gesture told the animals, on cue, that it was time to get going faster. Suddenly it happened. Mach Magic's strides grew in length and timing. The group of mares completed the last turn and headed for the finish. Our big girl not only held the lead, she pulled away.

My chest felt full, yet my breathing was irregular. Mach Magic, daughter of Illusionist and sired by Mach Three, was our baby. We'd been there since her birth. Now, at well over one thousand pounds of racing glory, she made me feel like my heart would burst open.

Magic crossed the finish line three lengths ahead of second place. At this juncture in her career, in her third season racing, she'd won 18 percent of her starts. Mother Lusi, our champion, had won 31 percent in her six-year career. Magic was catching up. Tonight's victory marked her second win under Tony's guidance. The fact that Magic was a bona fide Standardbred athlete—racing and often landing in the top five or top three—warranted attention outside of our family circle. Standardbred Canada acknowledged in a brief online article that same evening that she'd banked just shy of $100,000 to date.

I wondered if the horse somehow knew of the recent bills at the farm. The win tonight had filled the new financial gap caused by the pump and the pipe.

As for young Albert, it looked like the fall would be his time to launch onto the track—at least that's what Dave thought. I wasn't so sure but always felt hopeful. My visions of Albert racing never faded. In fact, they came to me each night, just before I fell asleep.

Lying in bed that night, the darkness made everything seem clear. I took a mental inventory of the herd. I rewound Magic's race and recent victory, and also considered Albert's prospects. Then my thoughts shifted to our horses at Hillsborough Stables.

Pan and Shorty were healthy and continuing to enjoy their well-earned life of happy retirement. Oldest sister Lido Magic and her baby, She's Magic, were still enjoying mare-and-foal time together. The filly's sculpted, starless face and strong neck sat above a more than solid body, and her two short white socks on both left legs—they revealed themselves to us shortly after her birth—guaranteed that I'd always recognize her in a herd or a post parade one day. In mid-August, Sheshe turned six months old, and the time to separate mare and foal loomed close.

Meanwhile, Lido radiated health in her second pregnancy. We'd chosen sire He's Watching again, since the genetic cross had proven fruitful in Sheshe's case. A full sibling was due in 2018 sometime near Valentine's Day.

And then there was Queen Lusi. Lately her demeanour had changed—at least toward me. She was pinning her ears and snaking her head less. My ongoing struggle to learn and speak the language of horse seemed to be lessening, because when I took trips up to the farm alone, Lusi shared moments with me that I'd never dreamed possible in the past. I wasn't totally confident in her presence, but there was little doubt that the Queen and in fact the entire herd were becoming more accepting of me.

Sleep approached, and I crossed my fingers that my new bond with Lusi and the herd would continue to strengthen. But I certainly wasn't prepared for the breakthrough that was about to happen.

As I advanced up the driveway barely two weeks later, I noticed a slew of fresh wooden posts and laterals spread out across the farm. Dave had acted upon Darlene's request to create more mare-and-foal-friendly spaces by swapping out the majority of electrically charged fences for a sturdy cedar option. The long stretch of fence line along Pan and Shorty's orchard-filled paddock ran parallel to the farm driveway. I slowed to a crawl and rolled down my window. The boys greeted me with welcome nickers, and then went back to eating the odd fallen apple. I parked in front of the barn and headed across the gravel lot to the big paddock near the road. My sights were set on one horse: Lusi.

Birdsong filled the air. In the warm sun of the early morning hours with the dew barely gone, there we stood— alone together in the vast, open space. Until now, I'd rarely spent time with Lusi outside. We'd mostly hung out at the threshold of her stall. These days, I made a point to catch my girl early, and today I'd arrived just before 9:00 a.m. Standing close beside her imposing figure, our legs rooted in the cool grass, I felt her coat bouncing sunlight into my face. I reached out both hands and ran them gently along her neck and back. My new grooming kit sat nearby.

"You're beautiful." I let my fingertips slide across her body as if I were reading braille. "I love you."

Despite having been a racehorse owner for years, I hadn't grown up with horses, so I'd always lacked the confidence to try grooming one—until today. I reached into the bucket and found the perfect implement. Using a rubber curry was the first step in grooming a horse, or so it was explained in a handful of videos I'd recently watched on YouTube. Lusi was covered in a blanket of semi-dried mud, especially on her right side. I strapped the curry comb to my palm and, starting high on her neck, I rubbed in short circles. The firmness of my touch and the comb's rubber nubs made loose, dead skin and caked-on bits of dirt fly from her coat.

Lusi pushed her neck and body against the tool, which put her so much closer to me. I slipped her a small piece of peanut butter bar to please her and help keep her attention on the task. Her eyes gave me a slow blink. The combination of the treat and my grooming technique seemed to put her in a heavenly state. The scent of peanut butter came wafting toward me as her tongue started whipping about, and Lusi's own scent—the sweet odour of horse—was unmistakably earthy and fresh.

I'd never known Lusi to be so cooperative and relaxed. I was used to being ignored or bossed around by her, always on my guard in case I pissed her off in some way. In the past, I'd seen her kick a groom once in the gut and nearly take the kneecap off a curious youngster visiting the training barn. He got too close and startled her, and Lusi's back right hoof came flying out. One more inch and we'd have needed an ambulance. I felt I always walked a tight rope with her, although I'd never personally been targeted. But today, together in that patch of grass, we were enjoying the moment. My past memories of uncertainty and fear floated away.

Next, I pulled out the oval body brush with its short bristles. I kept track of her hind end by resting my left hand near her hip and brushing her with my right. Carefully I brushed in the same direction that her hair grew, and more loosened dirt left her coat. The bristles must have felt good, because she signalled when I hit a favourite spot by moving her body to keep the brush in place a little longer. Perhaps I was relieving her of some itch, especially between the ears and on her star.

Except for her hind white socks and white star, Lusi's coat was dark bay. When I brushed her forehead, just above the eyes, I noticed she had a number of grey hairs beyond the circumference of her star. The shedding intensified and let go in a grey-and-white-hair shower. A light morning breeze carried bay and grey hairs a short distance before they fell to the ground; I was careful not to work directly in the hairy path. Lusi took a deep breath and let out an enthusiastic sound that was more whinny than nicker. I laughed out one of my usual caught-off-guard cackles. Suddenly she swung around, showed me her big behind, and gave me a backwards look that said, "Hey, no funny business!"

I switched to the other side of her body and repeated the process, working from head to toe. Her eyes softened in what appeared to be pure enjoyment and perhaps some forgiveness for the big laugh. With help from my back-up bag of sliced organic carrots, I managed to groom Lusi's entire body and take a few video clips. As I ran my palm along her rump, chest, and legs, I admired the feel of her muscles. Being so physically close to her allowed me to appreciate her soft coat, her size, and her strength.

Harder to appreciate, though, were the coarse hairs of her mane, forelock, and especially her tail, which all looked more weedy than lustrous. Long, thick, and gorgeous her tail was not, and it hadn't really improved much in the years since Albert's chewing fetish. My last implement, a blue mane-and-tail brush, didn't make it look much better. For one thing, I couldn't position myself in a safer location— standing to the side—because her sad tail was too short, and

I was terrified that at any moment a back leg might take me out.

Still, the time I spent grooming and bonding with Lusi gave our relationship a whole other dimension. Prior to today, I'd been a virgin when it came to grooming a horse. I couldn't wait to share this new experience with Dave when I got home.

The hum of cicadas filled the air through the open sliding door in the kitchen. Both cats lay nearby checking out the odd bird or squirrel that happened to cross the deck. I heard the garage door opener kick in.

"Check out my video," I said to Dave when he entered the mud room.

He squinted for a moment and moved the phone farther away from his face. "You're standing in the paddock—with Lusi?" His eyes fixed on the image and his brow furrowed.

"Yes! We spend our time there now." I smiled. I was feeling proud of my horse-care skills.

Dave's face stayed focused on the screen. "You better be careful." He looked up at me.

I jumped in before he could speak again. "Lusi and I had the best time together. She was so gentle. She even let out a loud whinny—or nicker. I wasn't really sure."

"Renata, a nicker is a positive sound—a sound of gentleness. A whinny is the opposite. Which one was it?"

"Well, the sound had a higher pitch, and there weren't any snorts with it."

"Just make sure you're safe," he said. "Keep your eyes on her feet and back end."

"I do. And Darlene occasionally shouts helpful tips."

Dave looked at me. "Really? Like what?"

"Like 'Careful! That mare can kill you!'" I said, laughing.

He just shook his head and handed me back my phone.

"It's okay!" I said. "I'm careful."

The breakthrough gave me such a high. Lusi. My horse. I groomed my horse. I smiled the rest of the day, right up to bedtime.

Because of my recent hands-on encounter with Lusi, I'd never in my life felt so connected to horses. It was time to share her story—our story—and the book with the public, although it wasn't always clear how the sharing part would unfold.

Chapter 17

BOOK LAUNCH BUZZ

When I wasn't spending my spare time with the herd, I was writing. I found out early that advice and talent abound in the writing, editing, and publishing business, and I rode the wave, which resulted in more than two dozen rewrites of my tale about Lusi and Albert. According to a handful of volunteer readers, the book had finally morphed into quite a lovely story about two lucky horses.

Although my manuscript had garnered a fair bit of attention from literary agents and publishers over the previous six months, their enquiries never seemed to germinate into anything real. I knew that the publishing business was in flux thanks to the internet, with small presses closing up shop daily, and that very few writers got signed anymore. So after countless rejections, I decided to take the self-publication path with *The Bounty of Illusionist*. Always on the lookout for an option within Canada, I chose a company based in BC. The company launched into my manuscript with an evaluation. It was generally positive, but they suggested my book could benefit from a copy edit. Fortunately I'd already found the perfect editor for my true story about horses.

This individual came to my attention through the Editors Association of Canada, now called Editors Canada. I learned of their website through an author who was writer-in-residence at McMaster University. Together, we entered two specific terms into Editors Canada's search engine—*copy editor* and *horses*.

Only one option turned up on the computer screen, a woman who lived in a small Ontario town and who'd been involved with horses most of her life. Later that night I called her. In her throaty voice, she spoke in a way that conveyed her high standards and her experience with both editing and horses. Within seconds, I could tell I'd found not only a talent but also a teacher.

Over a period of months, we concentrated our efforts on getting my manuscript into book-ready form. Our journey started with another manuscript evaluation, which was followed by a line-by-line copy edit: my editor looked at grammar, punctuation, dialogue, sentence structure, logical flow, and more.

Meanwhile, I'd paid the self-publishing fee to the BC company. My book was on the clock. The publisher's estimate for completion—manuscript to printed book—was approximately seven months. Extensions in the timeline meant additional fees, so the pressure was on.

A softcover prototype of *The Bounty of Illusionist* arrived at my door in mid-May 2017. My task was to scrutinize the text for any errors and to make sure that all fifteen images looked acceptable in print. A few photos were less than ideal and needed a tweak.

Now, with this last revision done, it was time to focus on the book-launch party. For the printed invitations, I chose the actual book cover image for the front. Lusi's deep soft eye twinkled at me, and her majesty wasn't lost even on the one-dimensional card stock. In the evenings after dinner,

Renata Lumsden

I filled out the invites. The final list contained more than one hundred guests.

I'd read a litany of information pertaining to book launches. The theme of the book tended to dictate the venue; for example, cookbook launches should be held in a restaurant. My book was about Standardbred horses, so Dave secured a party room at Mohawk Racetrack, for Friday, June 30. I invited family, friends, and horse-related folks—grooms, trainers, owners, drivers, breeders, midwives, and veterinarians, anyone and everyone listed in the book and then some. Guests would be treated to a buffet dinner, live racing, and one softcover book per family.

"Do you think anyone will come?" I said, eyeing Dave across the patio table. Eating backyard-BBQ-style on the deck always made food taste better.

"I bet we get about eighty." He sounded optimistic.

"But it's on a Friday before the Canada Day holiday," I said. "People could have out-of-town plans."

"Don't worry." Dave's face lit up with a soft grin. "It'll be fine."

A few weeks later after a long workday, I jumped into the garden. The dirt, weeds, and sound of a distant lawn mower threw me into a Zen heaven, until something resting against the front door caught my eye. Instantly I knew what it contained: my babies. I opened the box, lifted out one copy of *The Bounty of Illusionist*, and cradled it in my hands. I forced myself not to freak out with joy.

By now, more than eighty guests had confirmed for the book launch. Was I nervous? Of course. But never during the whole process had I asked myself how I would ever write, edit, market, and publish a book. I just knew that I would. So, like Illusionist before a race, I simply focused on moving forward.

The day of the book-launch party my stomach wouldn't settle. Dave managed to work things out with the Mohawk race office so that Mach Magic was competing in the fourth event on the night's card. Lusi's middle child had drawn the unlucky outside post in the nine-hole, but it didn't matter. The fact that one of Lusi's babies was competing on the night of the book launch blew my already blown mind. Who knew way back in 2014 that this night would ever come? It would have been lovely if it could have been Albert, given that his story was central to the book, but he was still a ways away from the track.

How does a whirlwind start? If I knew the answer, I'd know the origins of the phenomenon that *The Bounty of Illusionist* did not become. That hot night, nearly one hundred guests took part in a spirited celebration up at Mohawk Racetrack.

In many ways, I think now, we lit a spark that hot night. Passing out paperbacks to guests and watching as they sat with heads down scouring the index and reading passages that may or may not have contained their names, I felt a buzz growing. The one-in-a-million veterinary case that had had Guelph doctors working overtime to save our retired champion Standardbred racehorse, Illusionist, and Albert, her preemie foal, was now in print for all to digest. The attention the horses and story received in 2014 (and hopefully would now), while not exactly a tsunami from fans and the media, spoke to something larger.

My timing could not have been better. The birth of the book occurred as I'd planned, in mid-2017, which was not only Canada's sesquicentennial year, but also the year that horse racing and the four-legged stars of the sport, Thoroughbred and Standardbred, celebrated 250 years in North America. Standardbred Canada kicked off the celebration north of the border. The agency called upon everyone tied to the industry to commemorate special instances of horse-racing history or achievement. Article after article was sent to Standardbred Canada and printed in *Trot Magazine*. Among the throngs of storytellers, there I stood with my two-hundred-plus pages of a book, aptly named after our great mare Illusionist. I knew that I too had a story worth telling.

Phil Coleman was the first guest to arrive at the book launch. Illusionist's trainer from 2005 to 2009 looked like time hadn't washed over him at all since our racing days together. I couldn't resist hugging him, and the grin on his face filled the otherwise empty venue. Phil, my parents, and Dave's Auntie Marg made the list of folks deserving of hardcover copies not only pre-signed by me, but with an added personal note. Phil's eyes scanned the cover and then the inscription.

"Glad you could make it," I said. "You played a huge part in Illusionist's life and career."

"Aw, thanks! She's a great mare," Phil said. For a second, I thought I saw his lip quiver. Dave came over and gave Phil a big handshake and a pat on the back, and when I looked up past Phil, I noticed the line of guests ran right across the entire dining room. I saw the smiling faces of a horde of old acquaintances interspersed among so many new friends. It was my first book signing and I guessed for many it was theirs too. The contingent from Guelph and the vet hospital appeared in numbers beyond expectation. Congratulatory handshakes were exchanged all around as Dr. Arroyo and his wife, Nicola, introduced Dave and me to each newcomer in the veterinary group.

"How are Albert and Lusi doing?" Dr. Arroyo said. The sunshine from a nearby window cast a glow on his face.

"They're both doing very well," I said. "Lusi's the matriarch at Hillsborough and Albert's with the trainer."

"That's wonderful!" Nicola exclaimed.

"Yes, he's getting closer to the track," Dave added. "And Lusi is, well, Lusi." The four of us laughed.

As well as horse people, X-ray technologists, teachers, writers, and family rounded out the group. The presence of Dave's aunts and cousins and my parents and two sisters capped off the special moment for us both. They sat close by in prime reserved seating, and every now and then I caught their eye and they gave me a thumbs-up.

William Thomas also showed up; he was the award-winning Canadian author who had, via email, guided me on the matter of word count for the book and other issues. I rarely reached out to William, but when I had, he was always quick with an answer and some useful hints. He walked up to me in what now resembled a receiving line at a wedding.

I reached out my hand. "It's so nice to finally meet you. Thank you for your help and valuable insights."

William tilted his head to the side and leaned in closer. "Everybody thinks they've got a great story," he said. "Everybody wants to write a book. But you... you did it." He grabbed my hand and gave me a hug.

Our trainer, Tony, and his wife, Lisa, were there too, but briefly; they needed to leave to go prepare Mach Magic for competition. In a full field racing in the heat of summer, the horse barely had a chance from the nine-hole. It didn't matter. The bounty of Illusionist—Mach Magic—had made it to the track and raced the night of the launch. (One week later, at Grand River racetrack near Fergus, Ontario, Mach Magic raced to victory. She'd now notched a dozen wins in her harness belt.)

In our celebrations that night at Mohawk, one note rang through loudly for everyone: gratitude. For the horses and the moments we'd all been lucky to share because of them. Gratitude that through wins and losses, ups and downs, they provided what we now had the great fortune to enjoy:

friendships made through the sport, and heart-deep bonds with our herd.

While every family at the launch took home a complimentary book, some were kind enough to purchase additional copies until nearly one hundred and thirty were gone. Set free at the launch and through online retailers Amazon and Indigo, *The Bounty of Illusionist* was now ready to go off into the world and have adventures of its own.

Street parking wasn't my favourite. The memory of slamming a downtown parking meter to the ground in my teens had never left me. Driver's education class—specifically, parallel parking—had not been a shining moment in my history. Now I manoeuvred into a spot located around the corner from the bookshop, only lightly scraping both tires along the curb. *Whew!* A faint smattering of raindrops on the windshield signalled yet another storm, so I grabbed the umbrella, my purse, and the bag of books.

Bryan Prince Bookseller sat at the edge of the quaint village of Westdale, not too far from my workplace. Small by big-box-bookstore standards, the teal exterior with gold-etched signage made you feel you'd been transported to another time. I checked out the front window of the shop and marvelled at the well-laid-out display of mysteries, young adult novels, how-to titles, and a variety of colourful hardcovers and paperbacks. I knew my lack of authorial reputation meant this real estate was off limits. When I thrust open the heavy glass and wood door, a welcome hissing of small brass bells alerted others inside and briefly calmed my excited nerves.

From a row of schoolhouse light fixtures and ceiling fans suspended from above, a soft glow and a fresh breeze bounced off the soaring slat ceiling, also painted teal.

Alternating colourful spines and book faces reflected the variety desired by the community and nearby university. There was a noticeable lack of knick-knacks and decorative household items for sale. Exclusively a bookseller, Bryan Prince was known for providing a personal touch and a book-search service.

Frozen in place, I inhaled the scent of paper laced with a hint of dust. I knew this was a good home for my first and possibly last book. I moved toward the front register.

A tall woman stood at the cash desk. "My brother wrote a book. It was sold in this shop." She gave his name, the title, and the publication date, her voice filled with pride.

"We don't carry that item anymore, I'm afraid," said one of two staff sitting behind the desk after a quick online inventory search.

I listened to the exchange, grateful for the extra time to compose myself. When I looked down, I realized my paper bag with twine handles had crumpled. My nervousness had made me clutch it too tightly. Eying both well-dressed book-store staff behind the cash, I felt beads of sweat forming on my brow. One must be Andrew and the other one Frank—I couldn't recall which was which. I'd met them briefly in the past and knew their voices from phone conversations. To me they oozed the literary sophistication of people who spent their lives reading and appreciating great writing.

"I see. Well, thank you," the woman said. The bells went off again as she exited.

My tongue suddenly felt swollen, and I couldn't even recall the name of my book. All I could do was grin. Andrew's and Frank's faces lit up and brought order to my jumbled thoughts.

"I got a call from Andrew." I felt my spine straighten—a habit when I was trying to look nonchalant.

Renata Lumsden

"Hi, Renata." Andrew reached down and pulled out a calculator from behind the counter.

"I understand the Hamilton Public Library bought all of my books," I said. My face and neck felt feverish. Hearing my own words in a sentence I'd never strung together before made my heartbeat quicken. I could feel my shirt stick to the sweaty patch between my shoulders. Oh the joys of being a new author over fifty! I took some deep breaths.

"Four books in total," Andrew said. "Did you bring replacements?"

Recovered from the brief episode, I dropped the paper bag on the counter. "Three books as requested," I said. The last time I'd checked the library online, there were thirty-six holds on the book with all four copies out on loan. One reader had even gone to the trouble of posting a review. The person had obviously read the book because their words spoke to my personal, emotional approach; they gave it a five-star rating.

The whole experience—book sales and reviews— brought with it a mix of both seriousness and fun. I felt humbled, grateful, and excited. I'd even started receiving emails from strangers who loved the book and wanted to meet Lusi and Albert in person, although Dave and I didn't think we could accommodate them without disturbing Tony, Darlene, and Derrick.

With a ding, the till opened and Andrew slid the calculator over. Frank nodded and reached inside. My head spun. Was I getting paid? Oh my God! My breathing almost stopped.

"Thank you." Robotically, I took the bills Frank offered, opened my purse, and jammed the money inside without stopping to pull out my wallet. *These guys just paid me for my book.*

Outside, I let the rain pelt my face for a few minutes before I unfolded the umbrella. My feet on the concrete sidewalk felt heavy because my head was spinning with joy. I kept reminding myself that the horses were at the heart of this. It was because of Albert and Lusi. It was their entire fault. Standing at the stoplight, I reached for my cell. A text message showed up from Dave.

Trained Big Al today. A slow mile was good. Plan on getting him on a schedule and hoping we can get him to races. Fingers crossed.

I hit dial. I knew Tony had been hoping to train Albert at the big track that day. Dave answered in the middle of the first ring. "From Tony?" I said. "So Albert actually did train at Mohawk? And he's totally sound?" The good "slow mile" Tony mentioned meant no sign of lameness, no setback with the ankle.

"Yes. Albert's doing great," Dave replied.

"At Mohawk!" I shouted, hardly able to comprehend the idea. A pedestrian standing nearby shot me a surprised look.

Dave laughed. "Yep."

I laughed too. "Good for him!" The light turned green. I took off with one hand on the cell and the other on the umbrella, which held firm despite the gusts of wind.

"Tony says our little preemie foal might see his first horse-racing competition in late fall," Dave said.

"No need to rush. December would be fine." I cleared my throat. "I love you, Dave."

"I love you too, Renata."

Even though I'd dreamed of this conversation surrounding Albert's progress, I could hardly believe it. I just shook my head. But if 2017 was the year that I, a novice writer, could write a book that people were actually buying, 2017 could also be the year that our miracle foal made his racing debut and joined his sister Magic on the big track.

Chapter 18

THE LEGACY BUILDS

A full card of summer racing in 2017 was coming to an end at Grand River, in Elora. That night in September, Mach Magic was listed in the program. Scott Coulter took her reins for the tenth race. Scotty had already won two races that night and was likely hoping for a win trifecta. Nine talented horses waited for the starter's signal. Bugs darted about the track lighting as the wall of mares began to line up and head toward the moving gate.

With the cell phone cradled in Dave's hand, the real-time video rolled. "She has a chance from the four-hole," Dave said.

"I can't watch." I took off up the stairs. "Let me know how she does."

"Okay," he shouted, before things went silent.

Settled in my office chair, I hit Return on the computer and the screen came to life. *Lusi's Legacy* popped up, the sequel to *The Bounty of Illusionist*. The page opened to where I'd last stopped writing. I listened for a few seconds before I started typing, then whispered, "Go, Magic, go." The sound of the keyboard helped calm my pre-race jitters.

Stomp. Stomp. Stomp. Dave's feet on the stairs signalled the race might be over. Before I could inquire, he called out, "I knew it. God!" His voice boomed across the house.

I jumped up and headed out of my office. "What happened?" I yelled, standing in an empty kitchen. "Where are you?"

"I'm going to run around the block," Dave said. He peeked out from the mud room still dressed in his shorts and T-shirt.

"Are you serious? Is Magic okay?" I said.

Dave met me in the hallway and his excited eyes were hard to read.

"I want to do a victory lap! She dominated, Renata." Dave grinned. "Scotty didn't even pull the ear plugs." He laughed. "She was gone!"

"Really!" I felt my shoulders relax. "Let's go watch the replay."

"I told you the basement was a lucky place to watch the race," Dave said. He led the way downstairs.

The giant television screen still showed Grand River Raceway with its massive stone-block-and-glass grandstand. The venue offered Standardbred racing from June to September. The replay for Magic's race hadn't yet come up.

"The TV feed is always behind." Dave sat and I joined him.

"Remember when Lusi raced at Grand River?" I said. "Didn't she come third in a big race for three-year-olds?"

"Uh-huh. That race is still held there. It's called the Gold Series."

"And she came first in another big race that same year. What was that?"

"The Grassroots. Not many mares at that age race in both stakes races."

"Lusi. Our champion. Magic has her talent too."

The video feed came up on Dave's phone. Mach Magic led from the first quarter pole right through until the only competition was for second. The last four horses in the race crossed the finish line ten or more lengths behind our five-year-old filly.

"She paced great!" I said.

Dave grabbed my hand and squeezed. "Magic achieved something special tonight."

"What do you mean?" I watched his face admire the horse on the screen.

"The purse tonight officially pushes her earnings above the $100,000 threshold. Not all mares earn that amount."

"She's the first of Lusi's babies to push past six figures," I said.

Dave grinned. "It's a feather in Lusi's cap too, as dam, and Mach Three's as sire—it's a shame he isn't still alive."

I nodded. "Magic might race a few more years. Her earnings are going to make her an attractive broodmare and increase the potential of her babies." Wow, I thought: I'd come so far in my understanding of the horses and the complexity of this sport.

After our experience winning with Lusi, we knew that it took equal amounts of good luck, good breeding, and great desire on the part of the horse to succeed in harness racing. But Dave and I weren't searching for a Standardbred ATM, just a slice of the competition pie: a fair share of winning—and enjoyment by horse and owner—would be much more than fine. Mach Magic was providing that.

"I wouldn't be surprised if the phone rings this week," Dave said. He tilted his head toward me.

"Phone?" My confusion didn't seem to faze him.

"With offers. To buy Magic." His eyes met mine.

"Buy her!" I took a deep, exasperated breath.

"She's not for sale," he said.

"That's right. She belongs with our family."

There. I'd said it. Out loud. Not *our herd*, not even *our herd family*, but *our family*. I glanced at Dave, wondering how he'd react.

He just smiled and said, "Yep. She's our baby."

The next morning, we both launched out of the house well before nine, ready for a full workday ahead.

Just before noon, as I was in the middle of answering student emails, a text message bubbled up with a *bing*. It was from Dave.

Tony called. Magic came out of her race fine. Just a little tired. Albert went in 2:30s this morning.

I squinted at the iPhone, wishing my eyes didn't need to read so many computer-related devices. Teaching was a profession centred on the black box and keyboard on the desk but thankfully not limited to office work. I liked to think that my strength and staying power lay in old-fashioned, classroom-lecture delivery.

The last part of Dave's message made me sit ram-rod straight in my chair. It read:

A guy called from Vegas. He offered some good US cash for Magic. I told him she's not for sale.

I slouched back in my chair, relieved. Dave was always as good as his word. Pan, Shorty, Magic, Albert, Lusi, Lido, and now Sheshe: the family was expanding. We keep them all, I thought, until we can't afford to buy bread.

Chapter 19

CHANGES AND CHALLENGES

The first Friday of fall 2017 came on like a heat wave. While Dave enjoyed chasing the little white ball, I spent the morning tapping on the computer keys. *Lusi's Legacy* flashed before me on the screen. The idea had started from a caboose of chapters that got cut from *The Bounty of Illusionist*. I knew the title might jump around later, but for now, *Lusi's Legacy* sounded fine. The second book picked up where the first left off, after Lusi and Albert had both triumphantly survived. One thing was certain about *Lusi's Legacy*—the sequel would end naturally whenever Lusi's son, Magical Albert, reached the racetrack. If he didn't, I'd have to find a different ending.

My visits to our farm and time with our horses kept me focused on my task. I enjoyed the long drives with Dave by my side, two hot coffees between us, and the road unspooling through the rolling hills of farm country. There was still so much of the story to tell, and the horses fuelled the inspiration I needed and drove me forward.

By the time a cool October came around, so much had transpired. Tony had confirmed one thing: Albert had a mind for racing. Teaching a horse about the sport was key. If the animal accepted the role, then it was up to the trainer to see if the horse had the innate talent, which came from the breeding, to make it around the oval track.

The slow and steady method Tony took with training Albert—the horse was treated and trained more like a two-year-old than an almost-four-year-old—soothed my mind. I didn't care about the cost. Dave and I weren't smokers and we didn't have any college educations, cars, or weddings to pay for in the future. Our horse children were our financial focus. So the timing of Albert's debut on the track didn't really matter. From my vantage point as a teacher, I knew learners came in all shapes and sizes. Working with each individual—or in this case a 1,100-pound horse—required patience in order to find out what method worked best.

Our young gelding had recently taken yet another turn up at Mohawk Raceway, which gave him a second chance to see the sights there and get used to the surroundings. Until now, Albert had seemed caught in an endless loop of jogging, training, surgery, and recovery, starting with his gelding surgery and followed by the ankle chip. During that time, his training had stalled. But now our fully recovered boy was once again getting close to actual racing.

Dave made it out to catch the training mile. He captured Albert, pacing with all four legs floating above the ground, on the video feed. Tony sat steady in the sulky guiding and watching all the way.

"Albert trained awesome," Dave said.

The three words strung together sounded like a foreign language I once knew but had forgotten. I finally recovered enough to respond. "Did he?"

"Albert can do it," Dave shot back quickly.

"I know. Let's hope he keeps on going this time." Albert wasn't even supposed to be here, and now he was making good progress again on the big track. This time it really looked like he would join his sister on the racing circuit, and possibly start earning. I had to force my skeptical thoughts away and allow the positive reality to sink in.

Meanwhile, Mach Magic, the other half of our two-horse racing stable, had earned more racing as a five-year-old so far than in any previous year. The purse payouts were increasing, which suggested a brighter day was coming for Standardbred horses and those connected to the sport. Racing had also returned to nearby Flamboro Downs in Dundas for the season.

It was Sunday. The night was calm and cool—perfect weather for our big girl, who didn't always fancy competing in the heat. Magic had drawn the two-hole.

Dave and I were visiting my family in Niagara Falls. Partway home, we pulled off the highway and into an empty parking lot. Dave called up Magic's race on his cell phone. The small screen and close quarters of the front seat made us feel as if we were right there.

"Look at her go!" I squeezed Dave's arm.

"Mach Magic got away in first place," said the announcer, "with Robert Shepherd aboard." Robert knew the mare well; he had driven her plenty.

"This is her night, Renata," Dave said. His eyes never left the screen.

"Here they come. C'mon, Magic! C'mon, Robert!" I shouted.

Magic continued in first place from the three-quarter pole into the homestretch. Suddenly the long shot, McCovey Cove N, swung outside and burst forward. With our girl in front much of the way, they duelled down the lane. The other mare reached Magic's neck not far from the wire, but Magic dug in, and it was too close to call. A photo finish was declared. We waited in silence surrounded by the light of the setting sun until the race became official. "Mach Magic took second," said the announcer. Against a field of seven talented mares, she got nosed out at the wire after leading from the gate.

"She needs a bigger nose. Like Albert or Lido," I said, trying to lighten the mood.

I knew that Magic had lost a handful of races by a nose in her career. But tonight's race was—from many points of view—a great race. She showed her desire and aptitude for competition. The other horse had tested Magic. Rather than give up, she had tested the other horse back, right up to the finish. First or second, we couldn't really complain after such a strong performance. My initial feeling of disappointment soon faded and turned to pride as the engine hummed and we sailed toward the highway on-ramp.

The newness of the fall season brought big changes at Hillsborough Stables—the loud kind that needed time to simmer down. Red, gold, yellow, and green dotted distant treetops. The changes in the leaves signalled the occasion. Weaning time had arrived again.

Darlene and Derrick started the day-long process of separating the mares, one at a time, from their foals, including Lido and She's Magic.

Each year it was the same: the mares were moved outside, and the foals stayed inside the safe confines of the barn. This year I noticed that some foals, with wet noses pressed against stall bars, cried out as if for help. Others showed their stress by running in tight circles around the stall. Meanwhile, outside in the paddock, the mares' ears swivelled, catching the distinctive sounds of their babies. Many whinnied back. Darlene and Derrick stayed close by, watching and listening while every animal processed the separation.

Lido made no vocalizations from the paddock fence and barely looked back when Sheshe left for the weanling wing. Sheshe handled the separation and her new surroundings with a quiet composure, and yet her eyes darted about with curiosity. I wondered if horses sensed the occasion in advance and did their best to prepare one another.

Eventually, the colts were grouped together, as were the fillies. Darlene and Derrick began to get a better idea of which ones among the foal crowd were more independent and which ones were less so. For a night or two, stall space was at a premium, so a few of the weanlings had to double up. Sheshe and another weanling named Jenny shared the biggest double stall closest to the arena. I found both of them comfortably lying down when I arrived. Their heads shot up when they realized I was there. For a few seconds they looked directly at each other before they both stood up and greeted me. Sheshe came to me first but Jenny was right beside her. They seemed to find comfort in the new slumber-party arrangement.

Since the filly's birth, Darlene had sensed that She's Magic was special. Her calm demeanour post-weaning made the foal stand out in her eyes. Darlene filled us in the next time we stopped at the farm.

"I must say," Darlene started, "that filly has a quiet, sensible way about her. She's reserved like her mom, not attention-seeking like her grandma Lusi and her uncle Albert. She's got her auntie Mach Magic's beauty too."

Like Darlene, Dave thought She's Magic was a good-looking prospect. Sheshe earned high marks from Dave on a checklist of attributes, ranging from conformation to intelligence to temperament, and she carried the genes of her sire and her standout grandsire, He's Watching and Somebeachsomewhere. We couldn't be sure what our weanling might bring to harness racing, but without Dave and me uttering a word, everyone knew this filly would never set foot in a sales auction. Sheshe was family too.

At weaning time, Pan and Shorty were temporarily displaced to a big back paddock so Lusi and her friend, a mare named JAB ELLY, could hang out in the orchard for a few weeks until the young ones settled down. Lusi seemed to love overnight stays outside, but I wondered again what she thought of all the commotion from the babies. Did she remember it from her past, and did she miss motherhood?

A few days after the separation of mares and foals, I started horse lessons. Lusi was my target. Grooming her had brought many new layers to our relationship, but something was missing. I had no sense of independence with my big mare. I needed help to put on and take off her halter and lead. I couldn't move her around by myself—from stall to paddock—without help from one of the barn workers.

But there was more. For nearly a decade, I'd tried to speak the language of horse with Lusi, whispering sweet nothings into her two big ears. I wanted Lusi to be as captivated with me as I was with her. I wanted her to feel a deep connection to me as the person who loved her very much and would protect her forever. Instead, she wasn't too interested in her skinny human owner; she was mainly interested in my treats. So I'd scheduled three separate sessions with a long-time horseman I'd met at Mohawk—a trainer and breeder who just happened to remember our champion Illusionist, her attitude and winning spirit, and who only lived a few miles from our farm in the small township of Eramosa. I figured that if I could learn my lessons on Lusi, then I could handle any horse.

"What time is your session?" Dave asked. The morning sun was still low. Pink and gold beams filtered between tree trunks in the backyard and lit the dewy grass.

"I'll be at Hillsborough around 5:00 p.m." I sighed. "After my four-hour shift picketing."

The privilege of living longer brought with it new experiences. Having been on earth more than half a century and having worked full-time for almost three decades, I had never been on strike or walked a picket line until that September. My colleagues and I joined teachers at twenty-four colleges across Ontario in rejecting the latest deal from the government and walking off the job. Medical radiation science was a collaborative program between McMaster University and Mohawk College. Faculty, like me, taught on campus at McMaster, to McMaster students, but faculty salaries and clinical education came from Mohawk College. We knowingly gave up our regular wages for meagre strike pay—meant only for those who actually walked the line—in the hopes of a better contract. As program coordinator for the radiography specialization, I was there to support my team in a united front. Deep inside, though, I hoped—like everyone else—that the strike wouldn't go on too long. Yet a surprise awaited me on the picket line, and it was horse related.

Walking in a circle for four-hour shifts sounded like a piece of cake, but it wasn't at first. As the strike dragged on, though, the picketing allowed us to form new friendships and share stories with colleagues. One of the picketers was a young woman named Christie. I'd seen her at work and said hello too, but I'd never really stopped to talk with her before. As we chatted, I discovered a fellow harness-racing enthusiast whose family had roots in the sport.

"In fact," she told me, "we currently own a homebred mare named War Filly, who's doing pretty well."

"War Filly?" I recognized the horse's name as soon as she said it. "Your mare has raced against our Mach Magic!" I said, laughing. "They even have the same sire." We talked some more and learned that our two mares were the same age, had similar lifetime earnings, speed, and wins notched in their halters, and had often raced against each other.

What I didn't know was that War Filly's name came about in a similar fashion to that of the great Thoroughbred Man o' War from the 1920s. Both War Filly and Man o' War were born during tumultuous and influential times in history, Christie explained why the past had a hand in naming their mare. Man o' War was born in the US during World War I. War Filly and Mach Magic, born in 2012, had landed in the Canadian harness-racing scene around the time the provincial government turned the industry and its people upside down. Being able to speak to Christie about our love for our horses and their harness-racing challenges and adventures helped pass the time while we walked those endless circles on the picket line.

Later, I drove out to Hillsborough. Tonight was horse lesson number two. Lesson one had included putting on the halter and taking it off again, but my practising between lessons hadn't gone too well. Speaking the language of the equine was much harder than I'd expected.

When I arrived, Lusi was grazing at the farthest end of her pasture, even though there was better grass closer to the paddock entrance. I figured it was because from her location she could keep an eye on her mare friend, JAB ELLY, in the run-in shed. Part of me felt relieved Lusi didn't break into a canter and come straight at me. Today I'd decided I'd start with a good grooming to give us time to bond before my instructor, Frank, arrived.

I latched the paddock gate behind me. With the bucket of brushes in my right hand, and treats in my pockets, I walked toward my girl. *I come in peace*. It's what I desperately wanted her to feel from me. Peace. And love.

When Lusi finally seemed ready, she stopped grazing and her head shot upright. No sooner had she set her eyes on my pail than she started to come toward me at a clip. Her dark figure grew and became larger and more ominous. I'd for-gotten just how massive she was, and I froze. Instinctively,

I put out one empty hand toward her. Lusi came to a stop, peeked into the bucket, and then sniffed my palm. I quickly produced a piece of carrot. The bonding had begun even if my style included a bribe.

I was still grooming her when I heard the roar of an engine.

Frank pulled in before I could finish my task and start practising. His long-box black Chevy pickup looked clean and sounded loud. At barely five foot three, Frank amazed me with the way he gracefully jumped down from the truck cab and didn't lose his cowboy hat. Dressed in western boots, blue jeans with a hole in the back pocket, and a checked fleece work shirt, he kept his shades on the entire lesson, and his mouth played with an ever-present toothpick that stuck out sideways.

"Hi, Cuss," I said. His name was Frank but everyone called him Cuss, and he never called me Renata.

"Hi, honey. How's it going with the mare?" he called.

"Not good." I looked down. "I'm not sure these skills are transferrable to me."

"What? What do you mean?"

I looked up and saw Lusi watching me. "I tried putting on the halter and lead shank," I said. "I'm afraid I couldn't get Lusi to buy in."

"Hell. You're afraid. What did I tell you about the horse sensing you?" His voice was sure but soft.

"She wouldn't let me." I turned toward Lusi again. "She has a mind of her own."

His eyes were fixed on Lusi. "Where's the lead rope?" Cuss said.

"Here." I offered him the shank.

Cuss grabbed it over the fence and entered the paddock. Lusi took off.

"You have to keep pace with the horse," Cuss said, walking with purpose toward Lusi. Each time he moved, the horse countered. Lusi changed direction and Cuss made an equal adjustment. Up and down the hilly terrain, under apple trees and along the fence line went Lusi. The "try to catch up to me" game she'd played with me on past occasions was on again, this time with a new human. I laughed to myself. My big bad bay girl's less than perfect behaviour gave me a distinct feeling of vindication. Inside, I was almost cheering for Lusi to wear Cuss out completely. This round, however, only lasted for about five minutes.

"Like this, honey," Cuss said. In the corner of the paddock Lusi just stopped, or maybe she gave up. Cuss moved in closer. No sooner had he reached Lusi than he quickly slipped her nose through the halter and lifted it up over her ears before he fastened it. Then he unfastened the halter and removed it. "On and off. You see?" He repeated the process and then let me do it a few times. With the halter on and the lead rope attached, I walked Lusi throughout the paddock while JAB ELLY watched us. I practised stop and start, and Lusi even listened when I jiggled the rope in front of her and motioned her to back up.

I gave up on lessons that day. Between work, family (including the equine members), and my writing, it wasn't likely that the hands-on horse lessons and the practice needed would see much traction. I told Cuss we might try again next spring, but not with Lusi. I needed an easier practice partner—like maybe a very old, very obliging Shetland pony.

Besides, on top of all my other commitments, I had a book to promote and a preemie colt to look out for.

Chapter 20

LOSE SOME, WIN SOME, AND A BUMP

Albert had two schooling races coming up—one level higher than qualifying races. And I had gone through two book signings since the launch. Racer and writer were both moving ahead in their new careers.

The stacks of *The Bounty of Illusionist* sitting in boxes on my living room floor had dwindled from an entire fort of cardboard down to three. A combination of giveaways, mail-aways, and personal sales, led by book signings at Indigo and Chapters, had at least put the book out there.

The first book signing, at the Yonge and Eglinton Indigo in Toronto, saw barely a handful of autographed paperbacks leave my hands. I made a few faux pas that ranged from over-dressing to not nailing down my one-minute elevator pitch in advance. But once I'd learned those lessons, book signings that followed saw numbers more than triple.

Chapters in Bayview Village, Toronto, felt like a home-coming. Having worked near Bayview and Eglinton in the past for almost two decades as an X-ray technologist, I found that the familiar surroundings calmed me down. Plus the managers and staff welcomed me and seemed genuinely interested in my book. Not too long after I sat down at the table provided, I noticed I was being watched.

A young girl, no more than nine or ten, stared at me from behind a stack of magazines. Our eyes met once or twice, but she always turned away. She finally approached hand in hand with her mother when my area had momentarily cleared of passers-by.

The petite, dark-haired woman looked affectionately at her child. "My daughter has never met a writer," she said.

Is there a writer in the store? I gathered my thoughts and straightened my spine. *Gosh. She was talking about me.* "Is that right?" I said and smiled at them both.

"Someday my daughter wants to write a book." She put a hand gently on the girl's head.

Still recovering from being described as a writer, I crouched down to the child's level and put out my hand. "My name is Renata. What's your name?"

The little girl balked for a second and then said, "Jennifer," in almost a whisper.

I smiled more broadly. "It's very nice to meet you, Jennifer." Her face lit up and we shook hands.

"This book is about my horses and my family." I reached for a copy and flipped through the pages, stopping at a photo in the chapter on broodmares. "Here's a mother horse and her baby. There are many horses of all ages in this true story." The child nodded and seemed to drink in the images I offered.

"I'd like to buy a book."

The mother's words interrupted the moment and reminded me of what I was there to do.

"May I personalize it?" I pulled out the Sharpie and opened the book.

"To Jennifer, please," said the mother.

The smile on the child's face as I started writing was almost more than I could take. I watched the pair walk toward the checkout, and I knew as a newbie to this arena that I'd never forget this encounter.

People often celebrate their anniversary by reflecting on the past, which is often tied to family, in particular their children. On October 29, on the verge of our twenty-ninth year together, there were no kids for Dave and me—never had been, never would be. No one extra to love, admire, and feel proud of. Yet this anniversary felt different from every other child-free celebration of years gone by. The usual twinge of loss and absence that came to me this time of the year hadn't surfaced. I suspected the horses were at the heart of the change in my sense of things. Dave and I enjoyed the occasion over a yummy takeout steak dinner in the dining room and talked about the horses.

Tony had loaded Albert onto the trailer that afternoon. Trainer and horse had gone up to Flamboro Downs racetrack. Today was Albert's very first schooling race—a chance to compete with other horses in a mock competition. In my mind, Albert's schooling race confirmed our commitment to the horse and the sport. Also, it meant that Albert had finally broken the surgery–recovery–jog–train cycle of his past and was closer to the track than ever before. If his schooling races went well, he would move up to qualifying races, and if he succeeded in those, he'd move up to real competition.

Tony told us that he'd secured harness driver Scott Young for the job. Friendly, jovial, and competitive, Scott had acquired the nickname "the Answer." With his experienced eyes behind Albert, especially through the turns, Scott would ensure a good schooling trip.

Dave found time in his schedule to be there to witness the event and take videos and still pictures for me. From the texts, videos, and photos Dave shared, I felt as if I'd been there too, instead of on the picket line. He told me that Albert's time registered 2:02 seconds. It wasn't the fastest mile on earth, but it was more than respectable considering the depth of talent in the field of competitors. And for Albert, it was a breakthrough. Our three-year-old son, by Mach Three and out of Illusionist, came last.

Dave explained the race in greater detail when we sat down later for our dinner.

"Scott took him wide, Renata," he said. "So the horse would have more room."

"Did Albert look good out there?" I wondered if Dave could sense my skepticism. Last place was last place, after all.

"He sure did." Dave smiled and topped up the mashed potato on his plate. "Albert set himself up okay in the turns too."

I took a sip of wine. In Dave's video, Albert's neck glistened as he trailed the field. I felt badly that despite the horse's real effort, the result hadn't been a better showing.

"He just needs a bit more confidence," Dave added.

"I guess so. That would help." I scooped up some corn onto my fork. "So one more schooling race?" I asked, trying to recall Albert's training schedule.

"That's the plan."

"How's Magic?" I said, happy to switch horses.

"She drew the three-hole for Sunday."

"Cheers to that!" I raised my glass in the air.

I cheered again when, on race day, Mach Magic got away racing in the two-hole behind Maxim Seelster and stayed there to easily finish second.

Albert's next schooling race took place a week later. Images and texts shot across my phone—I'd no idea Dave would be there, but he'd cleared his schedule and surprised me. The wet track meant that the races would be a few seconds slower. Trainers, grooms, drivers, and horses filled the backstretch barn at Mohawk. After the qualifying races were finished that day, there were enough entries to fill two schooling races.

Albert had drawn the inside position against the rail. Morning showers had cleared by the time the six green competitors in his race took their places behind the starting gate. Lining up behind the car was part of the schooling, or learning.

The field took off, and Albert got away in second. Driver Scott Young eventually took our boy around the leader in the straightaway. Overtaking a competitor was also part of the learning. Down the stretch drive for home, it looked like a first-place finish. Then Scott drifted away from the rail to what he would describe later to Dave as a drier and more horse-friendly track location. The move allowed another driver to sneak into first, although Albert picked up the pace and stretched forward. Albert raced the last half in 58 seconds and came home in 2:04 seconds. Albert's second schooling race time was slightly higher than his first, but even I knew that a wet track accounted for the difference. Still, it meant that Albert had finally made a breakthrough in his progress.

Second place! Albert had taken the turns well, and his gait looked good throughout.

I was thrilled with where Dave and I now found ourselves. All our horses were thriving. Our debt had dwindled down to a more manageable level, giving us some welcome breathing room, and we viewed our earlier financial hardship as the kind of sacrifice that parents made to provide for their children. In our case, it was horse children, though thankfully we'd never had to go to extremes such as not paying bills. Three years into farm ownership, we'd preserved the health and safety of our herd without any regrets or feelings of martyrdom. And as a couple we were closer than ever to each other and our horses.

But just when we thought things were going our way, the unexpected poked its head up again.

I was visiting Tony's barn alone the following weekend, and Albert greeted me standing in the crossties. The horse was being his usual agreeable self. Actually, we were having one of our fantastic loving visits. I was feeding him carrots and he was sucking his tongue. Visiting with Albert in the middle of the shedrow was like having a conjugal visit in the open with witnesses. I tried not to maul the horse too much, but my hands never left his body the whole time. From his forelock—which, in its shape and thickness, always reminded me of a toupee—to his ample, muscular hind end, I loved the feel and smell of him. Albert's thin red tongue appeared between his partially closed lips whenever we were together. I was grateful that trainer Tony and groom Nadine were busy.

Standing beside Albert, I bent to take a closer look at one of the white pressure spots on his underbelly. That's when I noticed it. A monster lump, five centimetres in diameter, on Albert's back left leg, on the inside of his stifle. The bulging, hair-covered mass reminded me of the Egyptian flesh-eating insects from the movie *The Mummy*. The black insects were known to tunnel through the body, often drilling just under the skin's surface until they reached the brain. It was all I could do not to let out a scream.

"Tony." I walked over to get his attention. "Albert's got another bump!" His reaction upon seeing the mass surprised me.

He bent down to eye the lump more closely. "That's not new. Always been there."

"Really?" I felt somewhat reassured by his calm voice and expressionless face. "Hmm. I must have missed that one."

"Maybe it's a little bigger, but Albert seems fine." Tony turned away to help the groom harness another horse to the jog cart.

"Next time the vet comes with the X-ray machine," I said, "get him to take a shot."

"Sounds good," Tony said, and he took off outside.

The trainer's answer had left the door open for hope: hope for Albert to make it as a harness racehorse—Albert the preemie with his bumps and tongue-sucking. But the image of Albert's lump stayed with me the entire drive home.

As soon as I walked in the door I jumped on the office computer and pulled up Albert's X-rays and vet-related emails from the past. Sure enough, there was a mention in one report of a bony mass in the stifle area of Albert's left leg. There was also an X-ray to match. I let out a huge sigh of relief.

Albert hadn't seemed distressed at all, and he hadn't had any issues with training. Feeling reassured by Albert's friendly demeanour toward me and by his recent ability to grind away training and schooling, I decided to adopt the trainer's opinion about the bump and lack of associated issues. Surely Albert must be close to showing us that he might or might not have what it takes to actually get to the big oval. The horse couldn't go on training forever; the end must not be far off, I thought. Yet in reviewing the X-rays, I wasn't able to let go of the idea that Albert might be best suited doing something else—another horse-related job—if racing didn't pan out.

The month of November came in like a soft pussycat. A breeze blew from the west and temperatures held steady well above ten degrees Celsius. Albert and Lusi's story had landed in print once more.

Thanks to folks in Guelph and a referral from the Ontario Veterinary College, *Horse Canada* magazine had showcased our story. The index caption read: "Save the mare, or save the foal? Owners opt for a risky procedure in the hopes of saving both." Inside, readers were treated to a page-turning article that revealed a happy ending for both horses and a glimpse into Albert's potential racing future, complete with a few images.

I'd made no mention of Albert's medical condition to the magazine when they'd called. Albert's bump was only noticeable to those who knew where to look for it. Its presence didn't seem to hurt or hinder him, so we were just keeping an eye out.

At the end of the article, the *Horse Canada* writer was kind enough to mention *The Bounty of Illusionist*. The acknowledgement humbled me, and I appreciated how the writer's mention of my book didn't distract from the theme of the article: horses were living beings and deserved patience and a chance to live and thrive.

The article in *Horse Canada* prompted more opportunities. *Trot Magazine* would be next to chronicle Albert's rise from a preemie into a competitor in the sport for which he was bred, and they asked to be kept apprised of his path to the track. Albert's training schedule—with schooling races behind him—would see the horse qualify at Flamboro Downs in mid-November. If all went favourably, Albert would compete in a second qualifier, a week later, this time at Woodbine. Once qualified, it meant that Magical Albert would have a "line": he'd be listed on Standardbred Canada's website whenever horse people searched his name. In short, it meant a christening of our boy as a racehorse. Dave and Tony had hashed out the plan. Everyone went on notice.

I didn't pay too much attention to the details, but I felt unsettled. I crossed my fingers hoping everything would work out where Albert was concerned.

Chapter 21

BREAKING STRIDES, MAKING STRIDES

A rich harvest of pine cones littered the ground. Tall, slim, fat, and curved, they dropped from branches high above like woody bombs, and the cold nights hastened their descent. Mach Magic seemed to enjoy the late evening temperatures. She had recently made the podium with driver Scott Young holding her reins. Tonight in a short-lived, late fall snow squall, she flew up the passing lane, missing the win by half a head.

All the way home from the track I relished Magic's performance and Albert's progress. The horses were keeping us busy. That night I fell asleep before Dave turned out his bedside light.

The next day, the ringing of my cell phone while I was at work caught me off guard. Squinting at the device, I could tell it was Dave.

"Our baby has grown up!" Dave said, his voice lifting at the end. "I sent an email and left a voicemail at *Trot Magazine*."

The call was a welcome distraction, allowing me to unbury my nose from the computer screen. Tony had secured a spot at Flamboro Downs for Albert's first qualifying race. A qualifying time that registered at or below two minutes was the goal. Most horses logged two qualifying races before heading into real competition, although some went to the races after a stellar single qualifier. It was up to the horse, trainer, and owner. The journey up to this point meant the owner carried all the bills while the horse shouldered the training and athletic progress. Albert's post position hadn't yet been released. Results of the draw, due imminently, would determine not only our colt's number in the race but also the size of the qualifying field.

Excitement and worry ran through me. After I hung up, memories flooded my mind. Albert lying limp and lifeless on the ventilator. Albert lying on the ground with his disproportionately large head raised, tubes snaking around him. The miraculous reunion with mother Lusi and then the eight months mare and foal spent bonding at Hillsborough Stables. Albert had gone from a fragile 130-pound preemie to a three-year-old gelding, 16.2 hands tall and pushing the limits on 1,100 pounds on the eve of his first qualifying competition.

On Thursday, November 16, Dave and I drove out to Dundas. Seven horses would grace the half-mile track for qualifying race number one. Magical Albert had drawn the two-hole, and Scott Young would sit in the sulky. Our boy was one step closer to playing in the big leagues, and the harness-racing community was watching.

Dave and trainer Tony had two things in mind despite the qualifying race and the media attention: education. Teaching a monster-size horse like our Albert how to accept the bit in his mouth—the small piece of gear that helped the driver communicate with him—plus the myriad of equipment, including the sulky, had been a step-by-step, painstaking process for Tony, and for Albert. Albert also needed to learn the give-and-go of racing—how to let another horse take the lead and then use his own speed to slingshot back around the one in front to be first in the pack. Also, the smaller tracks like Flamboro meant two trips around the big oval and more turns to master.

"He's getting the idea." Tony scratched his head beneath his ball cap. He harnessed Albert up and hooked him to the race bike. The horse stood tall and alert, and when the driver hopped onto the sulky, Albert headed down the shedrow toward the sunlit opening with a determined look in his eyes.

"He does have a mind for racing," Tony said.

"He's going to get his chance." Dave's eyes followed the horse. There was no bigger fan of the gelding—in attendance or on earth—than my husband, I thought.

As Albert's second biggest fan, I sat quietly observing the scene. Spirits were high among our small contingent of supporters. I watched Dave and Tony check their watches. I felt jittery, so I made an effort to practise mindfulness. The smell of horse and manure rushed into my nose.

We could not have asked for a more perfect day for Magical Albert's qualifying debut. Sunbeams bathed the horses and track in a golden light as birds floated nearby singing noisily. A ring of light appeared to surround the field when they took off behind the metal gate.

Albert sat in the two-hole. He floated out with the others and lined up along the rail around the first turn. Down the straightaway, Albert paced forward, keeping up with the group. As he set up for the second turn, it happened: his legs flailed, his head bobbed up and down, and he started to gallop. His whole body went out of alignment and he struggled to recover his pacing legs. Scott Young had no choice but to turn the race into a training mile. Albert had broken his stride, and it meant the horse would need to school again. Albert's first qualifying race, his first line on the racing form, had ended in disappointment and worry.

I stood in the background. Quiet.

"He's a little rough gaited," Scott said.

"He's still learning," Dave muttered, his expectations dashed.

"Yeah," Tony agreed. He unhooked Albert from the bike and looked the horse over. "Albert's okay physically." He took off down the shedrow with Albert, Dave, and me in tow.

"I hope going off stride hasn't hurt his confidence," Dave said.

"Yeah, I hope not." Tony gave the gelding an affectionate pat as they walked along. "He'll get the day off tomorrow for sure. I'll check him again and then give you a call."

Dave said, "In the meantime, if *Trot Magazine* calls, I'll let them know that we've regrouped."

The next day at Classy Lane, Albert's lunch sat half eaten. Those who ventured into his stall observed him coughing. Tony and his wife, Lisa, also failed to entice Albert to eat dinner despite offering him his favourite foods. They were left scratching their heads.

We were heading home from the neighbourhood bakery when Tony called and said, "Albert's not himself."

"Really?" Dave glanced over at me. I felt myself tense up.

"Yeah," Tony continued. "His bloodwork looks good, but not perfect."

"Let's give him the week off from racing," Dave said. "We don't want to sour the horse."

"Okay," Tony agreed. "I'll train him here in a few days."

"Sounds good," Dave said.

From that day forward, Albert became the focus for Dave and Tony. I thought about Albert refusing his dinner and I tried not to feel overwhelmed with sadness.

Renata Lumsden

Nearly two weeks after the historic strike ended on November 19, my professional life felt as if I'd awakened in the middle of a raging river. The experience of waking early to walk in circles from 8:00 a.m. to noon had somehow made sense. My newly acquired buns of steel from five weeks of picketing did little, however, to prepare me for the disappointed and frustrated students left out of the classroom and the mounds of extra work I had to catch up on. I plodded along as best I could.

Thank goodness Albert had bounced back to his old self, I thought, so at least I no longer had that added concern.

As the radiography program coordinator and faculty member in the medical radiation science program, I had enough responsibility to always keep me busy. At times, with a one-to-sixteen ratio, the imaging-lab learning environment felt like daycare with a single caregiver and guardian. For safety reasons, I never took my eyes off my students, but I trusted them and they trusted me. No one got hurt and nothing broke on my watch.

Thursday was my long, late day at work. It included a one-hour lecture to sixty students and then four smaller back-to-back labs. Lately, Thursday was often our big family day from an equine perspective too, because Albert's schooling and qualifying races generally occupied a Thursday time slot. Which meant I always seemed to be absent for the important moments in our big boy's life. Fortunately, an online delivery method for one lab had allowed me to attend his first qualifying event. That off-stride performance was still in my thoughts.

After the last lab was done that November 30, I jumped in the car. Driving along Main Street, Hamilton, I inhaled the fresh night air wafting through the partially open window. I pulled into the restaurant parking lot, and Dave showed up just as I killed the engine. We dashed inside and settled ourselves at a quiet corner table.

Dave pulled out my chair. "Albert schooled today," he said.

I did a double take. "What? Today? Where?"

"Woodbine."

"I lost track of the days," I said. "How did he make out?" I dropped my napkin on my lap.

"Tony called late this afternoon," Dave said. "I figured it was either good news or bad news."

My insides tightened into a maze of nervous knots. Going off stride as he had that day meant he would need to school again. Today was the day.

"Albert won," Dave said. He reached for my hand. "He won his schooling race."

"Oh my God. What?"

Dave relayed what Tony had told him and painted the vivid harness-racing picture I'd always hoped I'd hear about.

Tony said the track was tacky from rain earlier in the day. He also mentioned that Ted MacDonnell happened to be in the backstretch barn with one of his own horses. Albert's former trainer decided to stick around to see our gelding go. Tony and Ted stood back and watched together.

The field of horses gained speed and took off behind the retracting metal wings of the starting gate. Albert got away in fifth. Jonathan Drury, a strapping young driver with a country-western look, sat in the sulky. In single file, the train of sulkies continued through one of the two turns at Woodbine. If Lusi drove with two fingers, her son, at this early stage in his career, drove with two hands, two arms, and both shoulders. Jonathan held on tight. Finally, he tipped Albert three wide off the final turn and then swung the horse first over on the outside.

"That looks like our boy," Ted said, his eyes glued to the oncoming horseflesh.

"I think you're right." Tony craned his neck and took a step forward.

According to the driver's feedback after the race, Albert had been "grabby"—he had the bit in his mouth and was pulling it side to side with his teeth. Jonathan said that he absolutely had to tip the horse out wide. If he hadn't, Albert would have ripped his arms off and run right over top of the horses ahead. Our gelding wanted "to go."

Once out wide on the last turn, Albert let the bit settle in his mouth. Jonathan was able to relax both reins, and the horse's strides increased in length. The whip stayed firmly back. Jonathan didn't even show it to Albert or thump it against the bike. With muscles popping, Albert flew past his competitors until there were three lengths between him and the second-place horse. Albeit only in a schooling race, it was the horse's first victory.

So amazed and pleased were Tony and Ted at Albert's performance, Tony told Dave, that they high-fived each other like a couple of teenagers.

"Albert did it, Renata," Dave said, smiling. He pointed at me. "I told you not to give up on Albert."

Coming down from work mentally and now hearing about our boy, I felt my muscles relax. I blinked away tears. With such a positive schooling-race result, Albert was one step closer to real racing, again.

At the table, Dave sent a short text message to Jeff Porchak, web director with Standardbred Canada. The story of our miracle preemie foal had first appeared on the front page of *Trot*. It seemed fitting that the magazine, through Jeff, would chronicle Albert's path to the track.

The next day, all room for doubt vanished when Dave got in touch with Tony.

"Albert came out of his schooling race okay," Tony said. Horses, like athletes, sometimes developed sore muscles or an odd swelling after competition. But Albert was fine.

The good news meant the horse was in race shape. The next step was a second qualifying race. It finally looked as though nothing could stand in Albert's way now.

Chapter 22

HOPES DASHED

On yet another Thursday, December 7, Tony and his groom secured Albert inside the horse trailer and drove up to Woodbine. Dave followed. At the track, Albert was moved into a stall. His mane shone under the overhead barn lights, and he radiated athleticism, according to my husband.

A little while later, Dave walked through the grandstand. He saw a friend, nicknamed the Pharaoh, coming toward him. They sat together.

"Big night," the Pharaoh said. "Qualifier, eh? What do you think?"

"Well, be nice if Albert started back in last," Dave said.

The Pharaoh nodded. "So he can see the entire field from there."

"Right. It's about passing horses and building confidence."

Flags whipped in the biting cold wind. The animals would feel the strongest wind gusts in their faces during the last quarter pole as they drove to the finish line. Due to a scratch in the race, the seven-horse field was reduced to six. The scratch meant that Albert would leave out of the four-hole.

The Pharaoh and Dave sat in the grandstand. The up-and-coming stars were listed in the program as follows: Ali, Summertimecruzin, East Bound Eddie, Magical Albert, Young Man Matt, and Sports Cowboy. Jonathan Drury held Albert's reins that night.

"Jonathan knows Albert well, right?" the Pharaoh said to Dave.

"Oh yeah. He's driven him plenty in training and schooling."

The wall of equine testosterone began to line up and pace toward the gate. The vehicle accelerated along the track, and each horse gained speed and pulled forward until the mechanical barrier whipped back in place.

"Look, that's him!" Dave pointed. The bright yellow wheels of Jonathan's race bike were clearly discernible from afar. Albert got away dead last and settled at the rail. The horses up in front began to shuffle off the turn. Ali revved up on the outside and cleared the field to control the lead just past the halfway point.

"East Bound Eddie's in second with Sports Cowboy in third," the announcer called out. With three horses up front, a gap of three lengths separated them from the remaining three. Albert held onto last place. But when the field entered the final turn, Jonathan took Albert way out wide, and our boy passed Summertimecruzin and Young Man Matt. Meanwhile, Ali pulled away in a commanding lead up front.

With his mane blowing in the wind, Albert continued flying first over on the outside. Down the stretch the field drove for the finish line. Our boy had second place. Just before the wire, Albert veered off the rail slightly, but it was enough to make room. Young Man Matt squeezed inside. In the end, Ali came first with Young Man Matt in second.

"Magical Albert made third." To Dave, the announcer's voice sounded like a far-off angel from dreamland. But this was reality. Albert had done it. Now, with two qualifiers in the racing books, Albert was set to take the next enormous step. Soon he would compete in his first real race for actual purse money.

"He did it, Renata," Dave said, when he got home that night. "He came third."

I let out a whoop of delight. "How did you feel?"

"Proud. But nervous. It's Woodbine Racetrack, Renata."

"I know. The big leagues. I get it." I couldn't stop smiling. "And he's going to be the second of Lusi's progeny to make it to the races."

Dave tried to speak again but got choked up. I reached out and hugged him hard.

Later that same night an article titled "Magical Albert Defies the Odds" showed up on Standardbred Canada's website. I set it free on Twitter and Facebook so that everyone we knew and all of Albert's fans could share the good news. A photo of Albert as a foal beside mother Lusi, with Darlene between the pair, stood out above the full page. Written highlights included Albert's difficult start to life and the risky C-section surgery for Lusi. Readers were reminded of the past, with a link to the original 2014 article in *Trot Magazine*. Compliments poured forth in the new piece about Magical Albert, who now had a pair of legitimate qualifying races behind him and a bright future ahead.

The written piece had captured the moment not only for harness-racing fans but also for our family, friends, and those connected to Albert and Lusi. The last paragraph contained an unexpected detail. With the holiday season in full swing, a last-minute Christmas gift titled *The Bounty of Illusionist* was suggested for horse lovers. I sat back with a slight sense of disbelief and read and reread the one page of happy harness-racing news.

One week later, it was time for us to let some outsiders—namely, the public—see exactly how competitive Magical Albert could be. Our boy's debut on the harness racetrack was staged at Woodbine. It was Albert's time "to go" in real competition. Dave and I hurried after work and jammed leftovers into our bellies before taking off to Toronto. The chance to support our once-preemie foal who couldn't stand, eat, pee, or poo on his own seemed like an abstract idea come to fruition.

According to the race program, Albert wasn't the favourite, and that was expected. But at ten-to-one odds, he wasn't the longest shot either; others were twelve to one.

That night the temperature held steady at a biting minus 8.5 degrees Celsius, and the stars twinkled high above against a pitch-black sky. On a fast track, a wall of ten horses in race number seven on the card started off toward the moving gate. Our big, muscled boy had drawn the four-hole again. It was common for me to feel race-day jitters, but watching from the distant grandstands, I felt my terror escalate to new heights. I glanced at Dave and sensed that his nervousness was also off the scale. I could only imagine what Lisa and Tony were feeling watching from inside the back-stretch barn. Knowing there were so many uncontrollable variables in harness racing, I tried to shut my mind off and concentrate on only one thing: breathing. But my diaphragm wouldn't cooperate.

Over the years, I'd imagined this night. In my dreams, Albert's first official race competition resembled a huge gathering with friends and family under a bright sun. Horse people from Lusi's racing days were in attendance too, from Toronto to London, to witness her son's debut.

In reality now, sitting alone with Dave—snapping pictures like crazy—seemed more appropriate and meaningful. Whether Albert came first or last, it didn't matter. Albert was a beacon of hope, I repeated in my head. His triumph over adversity as a preemie had given his life meaning. Whatever happened here and now, he would still be family.

I scanned the program. The race had been written to ensure competitors matched each other in age and experience. I noticed that two other entries were similar to Albert in that they too had zero in lifetime earnings.

I looked up and across the track. Even from afar, Albert towered over half the field in the race. The solid foal fed from a milk-filled blue bucket had grown into a massive athlete. His broad chest and muscled rump surged with power. Albert was going to a gunfight with a gun, not a knife— the trainer, driver, and Dave had seen to that. The fact that Albert was well prepared calmed me because I knew, or at least hoped, we'd still have a horse at the end of the race.

My feet kept moving, tapping the cold concrete surface as if motion meant things would be okay. Voices of strangers around us rose with excitement but meant nothing. In the reflection of the window before me, I could see myself and Dave. Our faces shone against the cold darkness outside like two white ghosts. Dave's hands were jammed into his peacoat pockets. Neither of us spoke.

The race had been scheduled to go off at 9:30 p.m. I looked down at my watch. It was after ten. My apprehension grew. Tiny snowflakes began falling outside, and the quiet void that filled the space between us was deafening.

"One minute. One minute." A voice rang out from the speaker above. The white truck rolled in front of the wall of horses. Hoofbeats pounded. The ground pulsed beneath my feet as the horses gained speed and launched toward the first turn.

"Something's not right," Dave said. His eyes were glued to the horse floating back to dead last. It was Albert.

The race continued. With each passing quarter fraction, the field sped farther and farther ahead of Magical Albert. When he finally crossed the finish, he was at least twenty lengths behind the second-last competitor and he moved like a tired mess. His legs were pushing on in perfect pacing motion but at a noticeably slow speed.

My eyes welled up. Dave stood with both hands pressed against the glass.

Albert felt like my child. Watching him move at such an abnormally sluggish pace, I wanted to run out onto the track instead of standing by helpless from a distance. For all the gelding's talent, Albert was known as a slow, sometimes stubborn learner. He had shown that he wanted to go fast, but he also had a mind of his own.

"Maybe he tied up?" I said. "Tying up" was what horse folk called severe muscle cramping. We both knew Mach Magic had experienced the debilitating condition a few times in her racing career.

"But tying up often shows up late in a race, Renata," Dave said. "Anyway, Tony will let us know. C'mon. Let's go."

As we drove down the highway and inched closer to Hamilton, the streetlights threw shadows off nearby vehicles along the sanded pavement ahead. Dave gripped the steering wheel with both hands while I held my purse tight against my chest. A few times a sob made its way into my throat. I sat frozen, unable to speak. We were only minutes from home when Dave found his tongue.

"Don't give up on Albert," he said.

"I can find him another job." I was barely able to cough the words out.

"Albert's a fighter, Renata."

Yes, I thought, Albert had been a fighter at birth and certainly during his challenging first weeks after birth. But competing at the track involved an entirely different kind of fighting on a whole other level.

"Maybe working with kids in need," I said. Albert loved people. He'd eat up the attention the children would shower on him.

Dave glanced at me. "Don't give up on him."

"He's just a preemie," I whispered.

Dave swallowed hard. "Yes, he's a preemie… He's more like a two-year-old than an almost-four-year-old."

"I guess," I said. "But what about his condition, the calcinosis circumscripta? Maybe he can't make the turns because of the extra bones in his legs."

"Renata. It's no surprise."

"What do you mean?" I said.

"Albert. It's no surprise that he continues to struggle. He's still learning."

We turned into our driveway and pulled into the garage. Dave reached for my hand and laced my fingers in his.

"Let's see what the trainer and driver have to say," he said.

"Okay."

"And for now, let's write the debut race off as a bad day at school for an inexperienced young horse."

I hoped Dave was right, because despite all those dreams I'd had about Albert racing and succeeding, reality had turned out so differently.

A text from Tony showed up late on Dave's phone. It read: The horse choked by driver.

Which meant that the driver had choked off Albert's air. But why? Dave and I were stunned. Something had happened out there on the track, and we needed answers.

Chapter 23

COMING FOR HOME

The next evening, the last light of dusk had long left the sky when our car pulled into the crowded parking lot. A dusting of snowflakes covered the vehicles outside the same restaurant we'd celebrated in a year ago. This gathering, on December 15, 2017, allowed us once again to pause and give thanks for the bounty of Illusionist.

Tonight, however, we were also hoping to find out just what had happened with Albert the previous night.

After the cold brightness of the street lights reflecting off the newly fallen snow, the inside of the steakhouse was as dark as a barn at night. I caught Darlene's high-spirited laugh and when I turned, I saw Tony, Lisa, Darlene, and Derrick already full of smiles and sitting at a table not far from the bar. Beyond them, the hostess and owner, her long blonde hair tied back, waved at us and offered to take our coats. Warm scents of garlic, onion, and meat wafted through the air.

"Hey! Merry Christmas!" Dave said.

Together we jumped from person to person, exchanging hugs and high-fives. The waitress filled water glasses and ran off to find a wine list.

Once seated, I wasted no time. "How's Albert?"

The table went silent. Everyone seemed to lean in slightly.

"He's fine," Tony said. "Look, I know you guys are disappointed. Jonathan blames himself. Last night, when he brought Albert in from the race, even before he handed me the reins, he said that he choked the horse at the gate."

Dave nodded. "Renata and I discussed it a bit last night. I told her you'd fill her in tonight."

"Yep." Tony turned to me. "The horse got hot and bothered by all the other horses. Albert started racing right at the gate. It was all Jonathan could do to keep from having a runaway horse. Albert got choked, bruised a bit, and he flipped his palate."

"Flipped palate," Darlene chimed in. "You know what you do for that?"

"The vet worked on it," Tony said, all eyes on him.

Dave leaned forward. "Remember when Are You Pan Enough flipped his palate? It happens sometimes."

"Remind me what that is again?" I said.

"The horse stops breathing for a few seconds during the race," Darlene explained, "when their soft palate gets displaced under the epiglottis into the nasal passage. The driver knows right away because they hear a loud choking noise and the horse slows down."

Tony continued. "Horses only breathe through their nose. The epiglottis and soft palate seal off their nose from their mouth. Sometimes, when the horse breathes out, the edge of the epiglottis will come up and flap around, causing the choking noise and interfering with breathing."

"I see." Because of my work, I could clearly picture the anatomy.

"Jonathan had to keep a tight hold on the reins," Dave said. "The horse's head was flexed too, which didn't help. Maybe we should open up Albert's equipment so he can see in front and behind—see the other horses coming? That should help calm the big guy so Jonathan doesn't need to choke down so hard."

"I'd use ear plugs too," Darlene said. "Don't want Albert to hear them coming at the wrong moment or it might get him going."

"I can't believe..." Lisa and Derrick began, almost simultaneously. He let Lisa finish. "... that Albert got hot and bothered," she said.

"Exactly." Derrick tugged on his goatee. "That's not like Albert."

"I know. He's usually so easygoing," Tony said. "It's tough to watch a bad race." He leaned back in his chair. "The horse definitely needs a change in equipment to help keep him calm and not startled by the field. Maybe even a different bit."

Finishing twenty lengths behind the other horses in his debut race meant another setback for Albert. Our boy would need to re-qualify in order to compete again. While the others discussed the pros and cons of various pieces of harness-racing gear, my mind was spinning. Like a super-protective mother, I realized that a huge part of me wanted to retire the horse on the spot and spare him the potential humiliation of another crushing defeat.

Seven days after his debut, Albert returned to Woodbine to re-qualify. Jonathan was aboard again from the two-hole in a seven-horse field—with a new group of competitors and a new strategy for Albert. Jonathan walked him a calming distance away from the other horses until the starter's car signalled ready. Horse and driver appeared to be in sync.

Tony had gone ahead and made a change on Albert's bridle, swapping out the blinkers for cups with peepholes on either side of Albert's eyes. Now the horse could see not only ahead of him but also behind, through the peepholes. The focus would be on the view in front, although he'd be aware of his periphery. Plugs stuffed in Magical Albert's ears would help drown out noises too. Jonathan could then disengage the plugs to alert the horse to the close competition and signal, at the right moment, that it was time to take off racing for home.

Before Woodbine had released the video replay online, Tony called Dave with the race details.

Frosted lace trimmed the edge of Dave's car window; it was minus five degrees outside. The ringing of Dave's cell phone was a welcome sound. Knowing it was the trainer, he answered after the first ring.

I sat quietly, trying to remember to breathe in and out.

Dave admitted to me later that he knew right away by the sound of Tony's voice that Albert had at least got around the track okay.

"Albert did good," Tony said. "Gapped a bit between horses, but Jonathan thought he was fine, and Albert finished strong."

"How'd he finish?" Dave asked.

"He was a solid fourth. The blinkers helped open the horse up so he could see the others coming, but the ear plugs meant he couldn't hear them until the end, near the wire, when Jonathan popped them. Albert seemed to like the smaller mini-bit too, because he didn't pull too hard on the reins."

"That's all good news," Dave said. "Sounds like the equipment change helped."

"And after the race, Albert's head wasn't down. His ears were up. He was standing tall as if to say, 'I'm Magical Albert.'"

When Dave hung up, he was smiling.

Later that evening, when Dave and I were at the dinner table, he pulled out his phone and we watched the qualifying race replay.

"Jonathan came to the gate last, so Albert wouldn't get hot and start to run away," Dave explained.

"Albert's in the two-hole?" I said.

"Yeah. The bike with yellow wheels. He gets away in fourth and pretty much stays there." Dave sounded like a proud father.

I couldn't believe my eyes. Albert made the first turn without losing a step. There seemed to be two groups of horses with a gap between them. Albert was leading the second group. The first group contained the race favourites, who were older and more experienced than our boy.

"Here he goes around the last turn. Keep your eye on him now." Dave's voice rose with excitement.

"The gap is closing," I said. "Look at him go!"

"He closed strong in 1:56.2 seconds, about nine lengths behind the leader. And that horse has gone in a fast 1:51 seconds at Mohawk Raceway."

"That's some serious race fractions from Albert." I shook my head.

Our "miracle horse," the gelded son of Mach Three out of Illusionist, had made it. Up and down, back and forth, it seemed it was never meant to be easy for Albert.

On January 1, 2018, the universal birthday for Standardbreds, all the horses in our small herd celebrated a birthday. Pan and Shorty turned nineteen. Magic turned six, and her older sister Lido turned eight. Little Sheshe had her first birthday and Albert turned four. Lusi celebrated her seventeenth birthday.

The winter came in earnest. Weather reports across Canada might have been slightly exaggerated, but Winnipeg was said to be colder than Mars, and Saskatchewan colder than the North Pole. Even in southern Ontario, temperatures plummeted. Mounds of snow swirled in the harsh, driving wind and scrunched and squeaked under my car tires.

The barn was quiet, and the scent of horse filled the air. When I got to Lusi's stall, I reached out and stroked her neck. "Happy birthday, girl." *Nicker. Nicker.* She looked at me briefly, then looked away. I took the piece of peanut butter bar and held it in my open palm. She turned and pushed her head through the door opening, and her lips stretched out to inhale the treat.

Standing at the threshold of her stall, I took a good, appraising look at my big bay girl. At seventeen, Lusi was still as regal as ever but with a tranquil composure and a gentle expression of approval, I thought. She'd slowed down, of course, since the peak of her racing career, although she could still move quickly out in the paddock, especially if another mare decided to have at her. The coarse white hairs that had crept into her bay coat seemed even more noticeable now, and they made the effect of the passing months and years undeniably clear. But her almond-shaped chocolate eyes still sparkled, and having chronicled Lusi's life in print—from birth to present—I knew our mare was aging gracefully.

That's not to say Lusi was any less discriminating about the company she kept. She was still fussy. Sure, she nickered more in my presence and would lock me in her gaze if I appeared on the horizon. Sure, she and I had more moments when we really connected. And I noticed that she was better behaved around other horses, especially her broodmare-friend JAB ELLY and Lusi's grandbaby, Sheshe. But when I asked Dave if Lusi knew that Sheshe was related to her, he thought for a minute.

"Well, I believe she has some idea," he said at last. "Or at least some sort of affinity for the youngster."

I was about to say, "That's sweet." But then Dave added, grinning, "What I mean is, I think Lusi might kick her last."

I always kept that comment in mind when I was around the mare. But on this visit I impulsively buried my face in her neck. "Hey, girl," I whispered. "Your son is going to race. Albert is competing. Let's hope he's got what it takes to be like his mom."

Chapter 24

ONE FOR THE BOOK

The alarm clock showed it was still more than an hour until the time I'd set to get up. I listened. The silence that filled the house was expectant, like a pause between thinking and speaking. I uncurled myself and rolled over, careful not to wake Dave. One thought controlled my mind. *How would Albert race tonight?*

Thursday, January 11, 2018, the temperatures hit a balmy thirteen degrees. The morning sky resembled a deep blue canvas dotted with fluffy white brushstrokes. Later in the afternoon, Mother Nature began washing away the salt and mud with a constant downpour. By evening, the temperature had dipped to nine degrees.

Due to the unseasonably warm temperatures and wet weather, the scheduled program of live racing at Flamboro Downs was cancelled. The combination of continued rainfall and slight release of frost from the ground saw the deterioration of the race surface in Dundas. According to the Standardbred Canada website, track officials felt that cancelling the races was in the best interest of all involved, especially in regards to the safety of the horses and drivers. Woodbine Racetrack was a different story.

The well-known oval of the A-track went ahead with its program. Racing downtown under the lights at Woodbine was a dream for horse people. Track conditions were listed at one second off and sloppy. Dave thought they looked more like two seconds off when he watched the opening races on his phone.

We discussed our strategy at dinner. Dave and I had chosen to run up to Woodbine the last time Albert raced. Both of us agreed that being there in person didn't seem to bring the horse much luck. Tonight we'd stay put.

"Are you going to watch?" Dave asked. He took a big scoop of homemade chicken pot pie.

"Nope." I took another sip of wine. Race nights always felt like I was preparing to board the biggest roller coaster at Canada's Wonderland. "You let me know what happens. It's his second shot at his first real race."

"I'll watch it in the basement," Dave said.

"Sounds good. I'll be in the office, writing."

Sitting at my desk, I was positioned directly above the man cave. At times, sounds echoed upward from a nearby heat vent. I heard Dave clear his throat a few times, so I got up. "How much time until post?" I called from the top of the stairs.

"Less than five minutes," Dave said.

My abdominal muscles crunched. I sat back down slowly and started typing. Black against bright white, the words hit the screen. For a short while my fingers flew and the tip-tapping of the keyboard was enough to drown out anything else. Then I heard it. The sound was unmistakable.

"Is it over?" I asked, just as Dave came around the corner.

"Yes," he said, in a low voice.

"How did Albert do? Is everything okay?" My hands poised over the home row, I froze.

"Well." Dave paused, and my heart sank. "He came fifth!" His voice rose. "In a field of ten."

"Really? Our preemie!" I shouted, and then jumped up from the computer. "I was worried because your voice sounded so sombre."

"I didn't want to give it away." Dave smiled. "He earned his first cheque, Renata." In harness racing, while the betting public was rewarded for the top three finishers, horse owners got paid for the top five.

With arms above my head, I ran and slid across the hardwood, back and forth, in my own little victory lap around the living room. Dave laughed each time I zoomed by.

"He came fifth," Dave repeated, a huge grin on his face.

In sock feet, I took a few more turns. It wasn't about the purse money. The excitement drove me. "Albert's a real Standardbred racehorse," I said.

Dave reached out, grabbed me mid-slide, and rocked me in his arms. I'd hoped and dreamed we would share this moment. We savoured Albert's accomplishment as parents would savour a child's.

"Let's go watch the replay," I said, and we hustled downstairs.

The details of the race showed what a good a boy Albert was. The starter's gate rolled on Dave's phone and the ten horses took off pacing. "Carolina Magic, the favourite, sits in sixth, ahead of Magical Albert," the announcer's voice boomed. Suddenly, a couple of horses behind Albert—Sports Tale and Overlord—pulled out and started to head for the front on the outside.

The race favourite, in front of Albert, pulled out ahead of Sports Tale and continued on the outside. Carolina Magic set his sights on the leader, Monty's Play. At the three-quarters pole, our boy was sitting in ninth. Knowing the outcome of the race made watching so much easier. Around the last turn, Albert looked good. Carolina Magic caught Monty's Play. The two horses up front sprinted into the final turn.

The rest of the field gapped out behind the two speedy ones up front. The window of the video feed couldn't hold all the horses because the entire group had spread out so far. Luckily, Woodbine floated each horse's post position number at the bottom of the screen. Coloured numbers jiggled as the race progressed. Number five, Albert, was in seventh. When Monty's Play crossed the finish line ahead of Carolina Magic in the video, Albert was in sixth.

According to the floating numbers below, number ten and number five looked neck and neck for fifth place. Suddenly, Albert, Jonathan, and the yellow wheels of the race bike re-entered the video feed about two lengths from the finish line, behind the horse in fourth, McKinley. Albert had flown past number ten, Sports Tale. Coming fifth, Albert had beaten more horses than had beaten him. Jonathan let the horse continue through the finish line. In Albert's mind, he was close for third with the extra burst beyond the wire. I knew that was all part of building the horse's racing confidence. Dave and I watched the replay again and again.

No one in the harness-racing world outside of our tiny circle was talking about the four-year-old gelding at Woodbine Racetrack days later. There was nothing special about Albert's finishing speed or the efficiency of his motion in the straightaway. But we knew he looked good out there, just like his sister.

In fact, a few days later, on Saturday, Albert's sister Mach Magic raced at Flamboro Downs in temperatures hovering around minus twelve. Dave and I jumped in the car and headed out to Dundas to watch. The inside of our car had

Renata Lumsden

barely warmed up when we entered the racetrack parking lot. We'd made it with ten minutes left to post.

Within a short hour, we were back at home eating tasty comfort food—hot soup and grilled-cheese sandwiches. No one spoke. We both stared at the photo between us on the kitchen table. In the picture, Dave stood smiling in his puffy black winter coat beside the driver. Mach Magic stood proud in victory. I stood close beside her head. She'd got away third and came first-over on the outside to win by a sizable margin. In between mouthfuls, we shook our heads at our initial good racing luck in 2018.

A few weeks later, just past 10:00 p.m. on January 25, 2018, the post parade marched in front of a sparsely filled grandstand.

The week prior, against another field of ten horses, Magical Albert had competed like a veteran. With Jonathan in the sulky, he'd stormed down the stretch drive to cross the finish line solidly in fourth. Dave was beyond thrilled with Albert's racing, and so was I. For one thing, the competition had been straightforward, with no unforeseen incidents or issues common in harness racing. But more importantly, in his previous race, Albert had finished fifth. Now he had finished fourth. We saw a positive pattern shaping up.

Tonight, I raised my eyes to the night sky and then checked the tote board; the temperature held steady at minus three degrees. Cold white clouds of breath shot out from each equine contender's nostrils. The frosty conditions didn't seem to faze the drivers or horses. Harness racing generally took place fifty-two weeks a year, although most horses only averaged thirty to thirty-five starts over the course of twelve months. Dave and I shivered, not from the winter chill, but from the thrill and anticipation as the start of Albert's third race of the year drew near.

Driver Jonathan Drury was aboard again to guide Albert around the track. Unlike for mother Lusi, who always had different drivers, not only had Albert seen consistency in drivers on the track, Jonathan also helped out in Tony's barn and had recently put in training miles with big Albert. The relationship between horse and driver had moved beyond familiarity and developed into a real connection.

Another contrast to mother Lusi, who rarely drew well in post positions: on this night Magical Albert started from the three-hole. Statistically, the three-hole start held promise. Although I couldn't read Dave's mind, I'd have bet he was hoping that Albert would continue to pass more horses than passed him. In a nine-horse field, a top-five finish under the lights on the premier harness racetrack in Toronto would be more than fine with me.

According to the program, the race comprised horses age four years old and younger and included non-winners of one race or those at or below $7,000 in lifetime earnings. They were listed as follows: Olliestrikesfame, Ali, Magical Albert, Bank Of Dad, McKinley, Larry's Petrock, Sports Tale, Your Raider Boy, and Prologue.

Looking across at the tote board, Larry's Petrock had the pre-race pick as the heavy favourite, with Magical Albert's odds sitting at a solid 10 to 1. Woodbine morning-line race selections, compiled by a handful of sharp harness handicappers, showed that our boy got some attention from all but one. Those that picked Albert seemed to be split: two predicted a fourth-place finish and two saw a little better showing, in third.

Decked out in race bib numbers and stable colours, the horses jogged about and waited for the signal. We saw horses we'd seen before. In fact, I realized, they were horses who'd beaten us before. The competitors were sleek and twitchy, often chomping on their bits.

Jonathan tapped Albert a few times to keep the horse moving at an easy pace. Our gelding held his head high—higher, in fact, than most in the field. With Albert's lifetime earnings holding at just shy of $2,000, the former intensive-care foal looked to me like he'd come to compete.

Before long, the starter called the horses to the gate. My heart rocked. Based on the look on Dave's white face, his did too. The horses began to line up and pace toward the vehicle with its one-eyed, blinking rooftop light.

The announcer called the race Dave and I had been waiting for. "Pacers in behind the gate for the eighth race with a purse of $14,000. It's post time." The sound of hoof-beats rose in crescendo. They were off!

My mouth hung open for a brief moment before I glanced at Dave. He was transfixed, anchored in place, with one hand resting against his chin. The rhythmic pounding of our hearts seemed as audible as the echo of an amplified bass guitar. I could hardly catch my breath.

Prologue made a strong start from the far, far outside and worked hard to capture the lead at the rail. The field fell in behind him. Magical Albert crossed over and was sitting in sixth. The favourite, Larry's Petrock, sat back behind in second last.

With Prologue in the lead and McKinley sitting second in the pocket spot, the two horses moved forward, leaving a gap of four horse lengths back to Your Raider Boy, in third. The rest of the contenders followed behind. Pacing off the turn, they raced to the first quarter pole; the speed up front measured a big tempo at 26.3 seconds.

And then down the backstretch, it happened without warning: Magical Albert burst out from the rail to go first-over.

I heard Dave take a big breath. "Albert's on the march," said the announcer. Dave finally exhaled and stood up. I couldn't move.

Four horses lined up behind Albert on the outside and proceeded in single file to try to catch the leader, Prologue. I knew that a horse in that position, first-over on the outside of the track like Albert, had a longer distance to run. I also knew that there was no horse in front of our boy. The ones behind enjoyed the advantage of drafting off his massive body. Passing on the far side of the grandstand, Albert moved steadily forward to the half-mile fraction in a legitimate speed of 56.1 seconds. Larry's Petrock was still in eighth.

As the group of horses went into the final turn, they did so chasing Prologue. Albert paced forward. He floated out there in all his hugeness, like a transport barrelling down the 401 highway. He was in fourth. Then third. Our boy battled on and I stared in what I realized was a mix of pride and disbelief.

Magical Albert had barely reached the sulky wheel of second-place McKinley when things changed. McKinley flushed out away from the rail.

"That horse McKinley jumped in front of Albert," I said, pointing.

"That's just racing," said Dave. His eyes never left the track.

"Albert's head rattled a bit," I said, trying to make a case for a foul.

"Albert's okay. He's learning." Dave's eyes stayed fixed on the race.

McKinley not only jumped out in front of our boy, but the horse turned on the jets and took off.

I sprang up beside Dave, who yelled, "C'mon, Albert, you can do it!"

McKinley was on the outside of Prologue, and Magical Albert marched along behind them. The third-quarter time was 1:26.1 seconds. Suddenly, Larry's Petrock got airborne and launched from the backfield on the outside. Larry was flying.

I grabbed Dave's hand and squeezed. We craned our necks.

McKinley took the lead with Prologue in second. Magical Albert still held third on the outside. And then, a blur of motion.

"Here comes Larry's Petrock!" Dave shouted, just as the horse blew by to take the win.

It was as if the rest of the field was moving in slow motion. But wait—with hobbles snapping, a pair of horses were nearing the finish line. Now the race was on for second place.

I blinked twice. The sight before me made no sense, yet it felt right and proper. From our grandstand seats, we witnessed a glimpse of racing brilliance, and a hint of promise for tomorrow: a familiar racehorse in a raging drive with another rival, each one bent on beating the other.

"Here he comes!" we both shouted. With his neck outstretched and muscled legs pumping, Albert was in total race mode.

He found another gear and his strides increased in length and timing. He battled on, but McKinley wouldn't back down. The two horses duelled down the straightaway toward the finish line. Albert stretched farther and fired a final burst. As we watched, the outside world fell away, and all that remained was raging motion, silence, and that incomparable vision of serious competition.

By a nose, Magical Albert had come in second.

Dave and I whooped and hugged and high-fived each other as if we'd just won the big one. Our once-fragile foal, the same one we'd cheered on to breathe, stand, and eat, loved racing. He'd finished his last quarter in just over 28 seconds. It was a heck of a mile.

My face hurt from smiling when I thought about the past few weeks. Upon returning to the races, Magical Albert had paced progressively better. He'd finished his miles in fifth, fourth, and tonight second against Larry's Petrock, a monster of a horse. There could be no doubt now in any-one's mind, including the handicappers and betting public, that Magical Albert was getting faster and stronger.

Over the next few days, Albert's accomplishments spread like the wind across Twitter and Facebook. Email and text messages came pouring in from friends and family. Words flew back and forth and the theme throughout was similar: "This was crazy. Where did all of this come from?" Darlene put it best when she said to Dave, "I prayed for moments like this but only dreamed he would be this damn good." Online articles by harness-racing writer Garnet Barnsdale about Larry's Petrock included a nod to our colt and Albert's won-drous second-place finish.

By harness-racing standards, Albert's performance on a cold night at Woodbine against a field of nine wasn't special. After all, the horse hadn't won the North America Cup at Mohawk. Our big bay gelding hadn't nailed a win at the famous Gold Cup & Saucer out in PEI. He hadn't captured the prestigious Little Brown Jug out of Ohio. But Albert's successes occupied a place deep within our hearts and the hearts of our family and close friends, who all understood how good the sunshine felt after the struggle.

One week after Albert's strong second-place finish, our world and his took another leap forward. Dave and I and the book went to CHCH-TV for their *Morning Live* show in Hamilton. There, I was able to spread the word to news anchor Annette Hamm about two lucky horses and *The Bounty of Illusionist*. Hamiltonians watching from home started texting us before the five-minute appearance was even finished. Work colleagues at Mohawk College and McMaster University—my alma maters and now workplace—had no idea I'd even written a book, let alone owned horses. Dave's phone fizzed with texts too.

"How did the interview look from behind the camera?" I said to Dave, as we trudged through the snow back to the car. The sun had barely lifted past the horizon.

"You did great," he said. He reached for my arm and helped me over an icy patch.

"Did you hear her?" I said. "Annette said that Albert was racing and *winning*."

"She meant that he was doing really well."

"I know. But do you think it's an omen?"

The day after all the local TV attention, Woodbine Racetrack had a surprise listed in the first race.

"Did you see the morning line?" Dave said, over his cereal bowl.

"Yes. Albert's the favourite. Unbelievable!" I had already seen the Woodbine program on my phone.

"He's earned that, Renata."

"I know. They base the odds on past performance."

"I'm heading up to the track after work," Dave said.

Staring at the morning line on my phone, I gushed with pride, and then felt my nerves go haywire. Watching one of our horses race live at the track always proved difficult for me. The morning-line-favourite news was yet another source of pressure I knew I couldn't handle. I'd sit this one out.

Chapter 25

SAVOURING THE RIDE

That night in race number one at Woodbine, against a field of ten Standardbred horses, our beast of a gelding dwarfed his rivals when they lined up pacing behind the starter's car. Albert took off from the six-hole and settled in the middle of the pack, close to the rail. Watching Albert tonight on TV, I felt fortunate to be connected to harness racing.

Devils Peak took the early lead and carried the field to the quarter pole and into the backstretch. With the wind at the horses' backs, driver Trevor Henry continued to lead the way with Devils Peak.

Watching from home with eyes half closed and teeth clenched, I did my best to concentrate on the moving picture in front of me. I heard the announcer say, "Magical Albert looked a little rough gaited in that turn." My head spun and the announcer's words whirled in my mind. Being raised on formula rather than mother's milk—due to Lusi's C-section surgery—hadn't stunted Albert's size. But big isn't always better, and the tighter the turn, the tougher it was for him.

Jonathan Drury had our big boy racing second over on the outside behind Prologue. Coming around the final turn,

Jonathan swung Albert out wide. With head high and legs pumping, our equine locomotive started to increase his speed as he headed for the finish line. White puffs of smoke flew from Albert's nostrils. Once Albert finally got into high gear, his mass and substance propelled him forward and his pace looked more like a quickened marching motion. The horse seemed to be racing with a military mindset.

I stared at the TV. Albert was closing. Waves of pressure ran through my spine and into both legs and arms. Would he have enough to catch the leader?

Barrelling up the final stretch for home, Albert propelled himself and Jonathan forward until his power-to-weight ratio reached its peak. The scene, for me, was nothing short of spectacular. Albert looked focused on the horses in front, determined to pass more horses than passed him. It was as if he wanted them to know that he was Magical Albert—a four-year-old neonatal-intensive-care foal turned Standardbred pacing machine.

I seemed to be hovering outside of myself. There was just enough of the rational harness-racing fan left inside to recognize that my nervousness had once again gotten the better of me. Stretched out and balancing on my stomach on the ottoman, like a human kite awaiting the next warm gust, I couldn't move. It was too close to call.

"Devils Peak and Magical Albert at the line together in 1:55:4 seconds," boomed the announcer's voice.

Unbelievable! Time seemed to halt as I registered what I'd just witnessed and heard.

The camera replayed the finish in slow motion. Both animals clearly knew what they were doing: battling to win a race. Tonnes of horseflesh hurled past before my eyes. The sound on the television got softer. I watched and waited for some official sign. Feeling as if the oxygen had been sucked out of the room, I glanced down at my phone for help. Social media exploded before Jonathan Drury had even jumped off the sulky. "The announcer shouted, "Magical Albert wins by a nose." The flash went off.

This outcome was something I'd hoped for but had never completely visualized. In the winner's circle, groom Nadine had her hands full managing Albert up front, while Dave stood proud between trainer Tony and driver Jonathan near the sulky. I could have sworn Albert was grinning. Dave certainly was. It reminded me that Dave was always happiest by Albert's side.

My phone sizzled in my hand. Dave barely sounded coherent through tears. "Albert won," he said.

"Unbelievable," I said. I stood there facing nowhere between the television and couch but couldn't seem to gather my words. Dave asked if I was still there, laughing and crying as he said it. He knew I was and understood my reaction.

Later that night, electronic articles appeared on Standardbred Canada and other online harness news agencies. Taking them in, especially the one titled "Maiden-Breaker for Magical Albert," I couldn't help consider how much in advance some of the content had been prepared. Did everyone else on earth know that Magical Albert would race and eventually win?

The thoughtfully written Maiden-Breaker piece began with colour: The yellow wheels of the racing bike glowed in the photo finish, and Albert's massive body shone in all its bay beauty, with his white pressure spots—from his first ten days lying on the ground—interrupting his coat in a few places and reminding those who knew of his story. With all four legs off the ground, our boy appeared to be floating, and he looked straight ahead, as if focused on winning, while Jonathan had his head cocked to the side, perhaps sizing up his chances at victory. I was already thinking about where we'd hang this momentous photo.

Tonight on the track, things had unfolded like a carefully choreographed gymnastic routine for harness fans to enjoy, as well as providing the perfect cap to the whole Albert saga. And thanks to this first-place finish, Albert had unknowingly provided a natural ending to my second book, now aptly titled *Magical Albert*. The miracle foal, born two weeks premature and kept alive on a ventilator, had demonstrated more than a right to play in the big leagues and pace around the big oval of life. But this, I hoped, wasn't an ending for Albert himself, but rather a beginning. My heart filled with a sense of wonder.

Around the time our racing stable was doing well, a Canadian icon passed away. The incomparable Standardbred stallion Somebeachsomewhere died after a struggle with cancer. He was only thirteen. The sire of Illusionist's daughter, Lido Magic, Beach—as he was known in harness-racing circles—had a nearly perfect racing record of twenty wins in twenty-one starts. In an obituary-related article on a Standardbred website, the owner of Beach was asked what he remembered most about the horse. He replied, "The ride he took us on."

In the midst of Albert's first-win celebration, I understood exactly where the owner of Somebeachsomewhere was coming from now that I'd had the pleasure of sharing a ride with Lusi, her foals, and her connections. Since Albert and Lusi's experience in 2014, the harness-racing community had lost so many equine icons—including Lusi's sire, Camluck; her dam, Mollie Hanover; and Mach Magic's and Albert's sire, Mach Three. Now the loss of Beach at thirteen years young made me stop, count our blessings, and vow to continue to savour "the ride."

Just over two weeks after Albert's first win, the bounty of Illusionist took another step forward. On February 18, 2018, Lido Magic delivered a 132-pound baby girl. The filly jumped to her feet within fifteen minutes after delivery, which stunned and pleased Derrick, Darlene, and us. Images they sent showed mother Lido in the process of cleaning the baby with her tongue. Fresh and new, the little one stood tall beside mom with ears up and new muscles taut throughout. At first she reminded me of Sara, but then I noticed differences. Despite being a big, strong foal, she was a little tippy-toed. Darlene said it was a contracted tendon in her front right leg. But the horsewoman assured us that all would fix itself in a couple of days—and it did.

I'd missed the birth due to other commitments, but couldn't stop staring at the images. A wonderful winged creature sat on the filly's face above her dark eyes. The unusual outline of her star reminded me of a honeybee. Known for their flight speed and strength compared with size and for their extraordinary capability to process information, honeybees had also been used by Napoleon as a symbol of power. I wondered if this filly had something different inside. As the clock ticked closer to midnight, Dave and I took in the images with hearts full of happiness at the latest healthy addition to our family.

The next day over dinner, we discussed possible names. The day of the baby's birth, February 18, 2018, was particularly lucky in my mind. A long-time believer in feng shui, I'd studied the ancient Chinese practice in my twenties and thirties after our failed attempts at conception, hoping to improve our chances by changing our physical surroundings to enhance our luck. I knew the numbers in the foal's birthday were considered lucky; now I just had to convince Dave.

"It's about the sound and the combination of numbers. Eight, *ba*, is similar to *fa*, meaning 'wealth or prosperity,'" I said, "and the number two represents balance and a doubling effect. Good things tend to come in pairs." I smiled. "The other numbers are kind of neutral."

"Hmm?" Dave tilted his head and continued to chew.

I wasn't certain if he shared my excitement. "How about the name 'Lucky Magic'?"

Dave stopped chewing. "Not bad."

"'Lucky' for the day, and 'Magic' for Lido and Lusi."

"And we could add the word 'Some.'"

"For Somebeachsomewhere, right?" A perfect way, I thought, to acknowledge and honour the new foal's grand-sire, who'd died a month earlier.

We both fell quiet for a moment, remembering the legendary stallion.

Dave put down his fork. "'Some Lucky Magic,'" he said.

"I love it." I jumped up and gave him a hug.

A few days later, Lucky, as we called her, walked ahead of Lido in the indoor arena. Dave and I watched and couldn't stop smiling. The filly carried her tail aloft as if to remind everyone that she was alert and present. Her long, skinny legs looked wobbly and awkward until she took off, and then they morphed into high-speed instruments of grace. With joyous whinnies, Lucky circled her mother, never farther than a few yards away, pacing out what seemed like her approval and appreciation of their happy circumstances.

Meanwhile, the maternity ward at Hillsborough Stables continued to see new life spring forward. The colt-and-filly roller coaster of foaling season had left the gate weeks earlier. One particular new mother was acting differently from the others. Her filly, born less than a week earlier, was her first, and the picture of health. But instead of making gentle vocalizations and cleaning and feeding the baby, the mare went after her daughter more than once, feet first and mouth open. The owner and midwives were shocked and worried.

"We could ship the baby out. Find a nurse mare," Darlene said. The owner admitted he preferred that the foal stay at Hillsborough. Darlene came up with a plan, which included us.

When Dave got home he told me the news. "Horses need a good home and a job, and foals need a mother," Dave said. "Darlene needs our consent."

"For what?" The running dishwasher had drowned out parts the conversation. I moved closer to Dave.

"To introduce Lusi to the orphan foal," Dave said.

"Really?" I stood still, digesting the news.

"Lusi's a good mother, so maybe she'll accept this foal," Dave said. He reached to pet one of the cats, which had jumped up onto the kitchen island.

I smiled, realizing the impact Dave's news would have on our mare. "Lusi will love the baby. I know it." And I knew that foals needed mothers to teach them how to be horses, even if they couldn't nurse from the mare.

"I hope you're right," Dave said. "I told Darlene to go ahead."

Just then I heard the *bing, bing* of my phone. The experiment had started, and Darlene had sent photos.

Standing in the shedrow, Lusi, eyes half closed, had poked her long nose and big head through a stall opening. Inside the stall, the foal stood alone, facing our mare with her eyes shut and her nose up.

Dave peered over my shoulder at the image. "They must be taking in each other's scent," I said.

The following day, I awoke to find a video. In it, a farm-hand attached a lead shank to Lusi's halter. Lusi followed her human companion at a slow pace around the perimeter of the indoor arena, while the orphan foal, named Nacho, leapt

Renata Lumsden

around her with legs splayed and back arched, unrestrained and full of life. Lusi obeyed her escort, but her deep brown eyes never strayed from the filly. On her way back down the shedrow, Lusi came to a halt in front of the baby's stall after Nacho had entered. Lusi stared. Darlene needed to jump in with some soft words and gentle urging. Finally Lusi moved on and settled back in her own stall.

Over the next month, the relationship between Lusi and Nacho grew. With each encounter in the indoor arena—now both unrestrained—and later with joyful gallops in the paddock in the fresh winter morning air, their bond tightened.

Dave and I took many trips to the farm to watch the bonding first-hand. At the beginning, Nacho would attempt to suckle on Lusi. Our big bay mare simply raised a leg and kept walking. When Nacho would fly forward without warning and then zoom round and round, Lusi would keep track and adjust her movements and position accordingly. Watching them from under a nearby tree or at the arena entrance, we felt like we were experiencing a new gift.

Because the little filly's real mother had grabbed the baby more than a few times by the scruff of the neck and tossed her in the air, Nacho had trouble getting used to Lusi's close proximity at first, especially out in the paddock. The paddock area also presented a challenge for Lusi—one with which she was familiar from her past motherhood experiences. When nearby mares craned their necks over the fence line to sniff the baby, their actions turned Lusi into something instinctive. Darlene and Derrick told us they watched our girl pin her ears and charge at the other horses until they backed away. Lusi was all about protection.

It's impossible, of course, to know for sure what Lusi was thinking, but Darlene, who'd seen hundreds of horses and foals over the years, said to us, "You know, it's those older mares, the ones who've had their share of foals, that are really protective and compassionate." And I believed her.

The next step for adoptive mom Lusi and baby Nacho included relocating the pair. In the back barn, near the tractor, Derrick dismantled half a wooden barrier between two adjacent, nice-sized stalls. With Nacho in one and Lusi next door, the pair began spending time together day and night. I'd seen the half-walls up at the Ontario Veterinary College and fully understood the concept. Between dismantling walls and hourly bucket feedings, the midwife team was all about the horses' needs. We could only hope that through their efforts, the bond between Lusi and Nacho would be strong enough to take.

Chapter 26

A WINNING FAMILY

While all this was going on, Albert was back at Woodbine. The first of March came in more like January. The winds whipped and temperatures plunged. Dave and I had planned to head to Toronto for a nice meal and then watch our young gelding compete. Our plans changed around noon.

I was writing away in the office when my cell phone buzzed. It was Dave. "We'll have to stay put tonight," he said.

"Really! Why?"

"Snowmageddon is coming. They're forecasting thirty centimetres from Niagara to Toronto."

"I took the day off," I said. I knew I sounded disappointed.

"I know." Dave sighed. "I'll bring home dinner and we can watch the race on TV."

"I hope the roads are okay for Tony and Albert," I said.

Clear skies, cold temperatures, and a fast track stared back at us from the basement big screen. The snow had yet to arrive at Woodbine. The starter's gate moved forward, with eight muscled competitors following behind. Each horse in the race was five years old or younger, and was either a non-winner of two races or had earned $25,000 or less at the track. Albert's earnings hovered at $15,000, and at the age of four he'd won one race in his career. Our big gelding held the six-hole with Jonathan in the bike. Albert was listed as the second favourite on the tote board and also by a handful of pre-race handicappers. Gerardo, the horse in the one-hole, was the favourite, with race-time odds at 3 to 5.

All of a sudden, just as the car pulled away from the field, the "Inquiry" sign flashed on the screen. Horse number two, IAMSAM SAMIAM, was gapped way, way behind the group. He hadn't gotten a fair start, but there was no need for a restart. The betting public would simply be refunded for horse number two.

The field rushed forward. Three horses seemed to float farther ahead than the rest. Jonathan came flying up on the outside and put Magical Albert up front in the lead. The first quarter was clocked at a very fast 26.4 seconds. When the announcer repeated our boy's name, I tensed up. Heza Big Dealer sat in second. Gerardo got away in third, with the rest of the horses trailing behind.

At the midway point of the race, Magical Albert led. He got a nice breather in the second quarter going a slower pace at 30:1 seconds. Past the midway point, Gerardo shuffled to the outside. The favourite started forward to catch Albert. I looked for that usual burst of speed on the outside from the oncoming competitor but saw something different. Gerardo swung out wide around the final turn, but he was only chipping away in his forward movement, catching Heza Big Dealer in second.

Down the stretch drive they came. Albert held the lead by one horse length. Gerardo was still closing from his spot in second. In the final eighth of a mile, Jonathan tapped the bike with his whip. This signal put Magical Albert into an all-out mad drive for home. I could see the length of Albert's strides increasing and the tempo of his strides getting faster. But Gerardo charged forward. Pacing for home, the favourite pulled up on the outside. His nose reached Albert's saddle pad. Only half a horse length now separated first and second. Suddenly, Magical Albert seemed to notice the competition. Our boy dug in at the rail and stretched his neck at the finish line. When the two horses passed the wire, the announcer's voice rose sharply. I heard him clearly say, "Holding on for the win is Magical Albert!"

I jumped up and raised both arms over my head, mimicking the touchdown signal. Being upright felt good after the body knot I'd been in while watching the race. Dave grabbed me around the waist and spun me around. We'd just witnessed another unbelievable moment with Albert, who was now being referred to on social media as the "Miracle Horse." Albert had a following, and Twitter and Facebook lit up.

Before me on the TV screen, Nadine the groom, Jonathan the driver, and trainer Tony, in his black-and-white racing colours, stood with our Albert in the winner's circle. I'd missed another special moment in person, but at least I'd seen it happen in real time with Dave.

Still, I had trouble comprehending the event. Albert winning his maiden-breaking race was one thing. But winning in the next class up against a field of substantial racehorses was entirely different. Albert had come home in a fast 27.3 seconds, and he'd crossed the finish line in 1:53.3 seconds. It was a new lifetime "mark," or record, for our gelding.

The race and win made me think of the last chapter of *The Bounty of Illusionist*. "Reflection" was the title, and I knew it from memory. The second paragraph read, "What did the future hold for Albert? Was he destined to make it to the track and win like his mom? Would the friendly attitude instilled in him during those first few weeks in the sole company of humans stand him in good stead as a successful Standardbred racehorse? Or would his precarious start in life come back to haunt us in the form of unforeseeable medical complications? Only time would tell."

Time had told the tale. At the veterinary college in Guelph, I'd felt tiny in the big building and dwarfed by the immensity of Lusi and Albert's medical dilemma. In retrospect, I realized that one bad decision could have changed so much. I didn't understand everything back then, but that's what made the influence of our equine family on my life—on *our* lives—so special. It's what opened my heart and mind to move beyond the confines of science and beyond the typical definition of family.

Disney movies and other media often glorified conventional family life by including in their depictions two parents and a handful of adorable children. But animals could be just as important a part of family, and they brought joy and love to all, enriching one's life and wellness to boot. After all, animals—horses and cats included—weren't lesser beings compared with humans, but simply different. When I stopped to compare horses with children, I truly appreciated the similarities. Children and animals both required a commitment of time, love, patience, and finances. The horses and the life lessons they taught us would be our legacy, through their bloodlines and my books about them.

Just as we had given Lusi the space she needed to be a great racehorse and excellent mother, she helped shape us, as well—as a couple, as animal lovers, as people, as a family. Lusi and Albert had given us gifts, which were both priceless and free. At first it was hard to recognize and accept them. But Albert—the struggling preemie turned bona fide racehorse—had, through his achievements, health, and success, erased the stain I felt on my soul.

I had believed euthanasia was the only humane choice for him. Now, four years after his birth, Lusi, Albert, Magic, Lido, Sheshe, Lucky, Pan, and Shorty and my married life had merged into one special thing—love. In a crazy way, I felt like Lusi had been nudging me in this direction and to this perspective ever since she'd come into our lives, reinvigorating parts of me and of my relationship with Dave that had faded slightly with our dashed hopes of having children. Through Lusi and her offspring, in particular Albert, and their gentle affection, I felt elevated beyond mere couple status. The horses had given me that: a sense of family.

Dave and I had each other, and that would never change, but now—so late in our lives—this miracle had occurred. It wasn't hard anymore for me to accept that Dave and I entered our fifties without children and that four-legged creatures and two books had taken their place and our focus. All these decades, I had coped with not being among the majority of traditional families by distancing myself from that group, but now it didn't matter.

A few days after Albert's second victory, a groom at Tony's barn informed us that folks up at the vet college in Guelph were using a new cell phone ringtone in honour of Albert. "Don't Stop Believin'," by the band Journey, was being played across campus to honour the preemie foal turned competitor. In this case, as in the song, the movie never seems to end. Instead, "it goes on and on and on and on."

Somebody should make a film about this particular journey. Quick, call Disney!

Epilogue

It's been a year since I finished the book, and I find myself spending more and more time with the herd and loving every second of it.

With an occasional spirited thundering thwack, Illusionist reminds us all that she's still the matriarch at Hillsborough Stables. Lusi did end up devoting herself to little Nacho for six months, and their bond was just as intense and loving as the bonds I'd witnessed with her very own babies. Weaning time went well for both.

Coincidentally, Some Lucky Magic was stalled right beside Nacho (Harley Z Tam is her racing name). The two fillies often hung their heads over the half stall door during our visits. They seemed to be communicating and enjoying some sort of young equine friendship. Both Lucky and Nacho became yearlings in January of 2019.

Tony's excited about Some Lucky Magic. He told us that this one "is all legs." Apparently that pleases him. We've already registered Lucky to compete in high-pursed stakes races for two-year-old fillies.

In the meantime, She's Magic has turned two. In barn four at Classy Lane, they refer to Sheshe as the "homebred" because the other horses her age there were all purchased at auction. Sheshe has picked things up quickly and is growing and filling out nicely, according to Tony.

Meanwhile, at 4:00 a.m. on February 27, 2019, Lido Magic gave birth again. Just like Lusi, Lido surprised us with a colt after successive fillies. This time we'd chosen Artspeak for the sire, so we named the foal Magical Arthur. After baby Arthur, Lido gets a year off from broodmare duties.

Are You Pan Enough and Shorty Bones continue to greet visitors along the fence line at Hillsborough Stables. Pan still acts a little high-strung sometimes, and Shorty gets into trouble biting things he shouldn't, but otherwise the two geldings live the good life.

Mach Magic carried our herd family racing and earning throughout 2018 and into 2019. At seven, she's raced more and earned more than any other of Lusi's progeny. In March of 2019, she came up lame after finishing third at Flamboro. The vet investigated and X-rays were taken of Magic's right front knee. Rather than risk further injury, we decided to retire her a few months earlier than expected. She did her best racing and representing our family from 2015 to 2019, and we couldn't be more proud of our mare Mach Magic. Derrick and Darlene welcomed her back home at Hillsborough Stables. Magic's broodmare career awaits her.

Which brings us finally to Albert. After his second victory in March 2018, he competed a handful more times. While he didn't notch another win, he often finished in the top five, including second place by a nose at Georgian Downs in Barrie. By June 2018, he'd earned enough to cover his care for the year. That's when things went sideways.

A small fracture in Albert's left hind fetlock sidelined our boy. After X-rays and an arthroscopic procedure, which also revealed some arthritis, he went back home to Hillsborough, where he kicked his way through his recovery time. Albert stayed off the track for ten months, but in March 2019,

Tony and the now five-year-old Albert started jogging again. There's a saying in harness racing: "The horse will tell you." My fingers are crossed, but I have a good feeling that Albert will soon tell us he's ready and willing to compete again.

In the meantime, I've reached out to a horse friend, who's in the equine therapy business. She's met Albert and, more importantly, knows his story. With her help, the word has gone out that Magical Albert might be looking for therapy work in the future. But whatever happens, he's our boy, and there'll always be a place for him at Hillsborough Stables—and an even bigger place in our hearts.

THE END

More About the Horses in This Book

Barnsdale, Garnet. "Buzzworthy: The good and the ugly at Woodbine." Harness Racing Update, January 2, 2018. harnessracingupdate.com/2018/01/28/buzzworthy-good-ugly-woodbine/.

——. "Buzzworthy: Waikiki Beach impressive in NA debut: Magical Albert magical." Harness Racing Update, February 2, 2018. harnessracingupdate.com/2018/02/02/buzzworthy-waikiki-beach-impressive-na-debut-magical-albert-magical/.

——. "How Magical Albert defied the odds." Down The Stretch, March 9–April 28, 2018.

Brown, Liz. "Magical Albert." Horse Canada, November 8, 2017. horse-canada.com/magazine/miscellaneous/magical-albert/.

Central Ontario Standardbred Association. "Maiden-Breaker For Magical Albert." Cosaonline.com. https://www.cosaonline.com/news/maiden-breaker-magical-albert/attachment/magical-albert/index.html (accessed February 2, 2018).

Coyle, Jim. "Racehorse owner had to choose between mare or foal." *The Toronto Star*, April 12, 2014. thestar.com/news/gta/2014/04/12/racehorse_owner_had_to_choose_between_mare_or_foal.html.

Ferrier, Melanie. "Classy Lane Stables rebuilds after barn fire that killed 43 horses." *CBC News*, March 19, 2016. cbc.ca/news/canada/kitchener-waterloo/classy-lanes-puslinch-barn-rebuilds-after-devastating-2016-fire-1.3497328.

Flanagan, Ryan. "Classy Lane stable fire blamed on electrical issue." *CTV News, December 16, 2016.* kitchener.ctvnews.ca/guelph/classy-lane-stable-fire-blamed-on-electrical-issue-1.3207138.

Lumsden, Renata. *The Bounty of Illusionist*. Victoria, BC: FriesenPress, 2017.

Mangione, Kendra, and Dario Balca. "'It's devastating': Community reeling after dozens of racehorses die in fire." *CTV News*, January 6, 2016. ctvnews.ca/canada/it-s-devastating-community-reeling-after-dozens-of-racehorses-die-in-fire-1.2723785.

McCalmont, Keith. "Survival: The fight of a lifetime." *Trot Magazine, March 2014.* standardbredcanada.ca/trot/march-2014/survival-fight-lifetime.html.

McQuigge, Michelle. "More than 40 horses killed in barn fire at Classy Lane Stables west of Toronto." *Global News, January 5, 2016.* globalnews.ca/news/2433586/more-than-40-horses-reportedly-killed-in-barn-fire-west-of-toronto/.

Porchak, Jeff. "Connections reflect on 'Beach.'" *Standardbred Canada*, January 14, 2018. standardbredcanada.ca/

news/1-14-18/connections-reflect-somebeachsome-where.html.

———. "Magical Albert defies the odds." *Standardbred Canada, December 7, 2017.* standardbredcanada.ca/news/12-7-17/magical-albert-defies-odds.html.

Seven Reflections. "What Does Name "Sheshe" Mean." Sevenreflections.com. sevenreflections.com/name/sheshe (accessed February 14, 2017).

Standardbred Canada. "Maiden-Breaker for Magical Albert." *Standardbred Canada, February 1, 2018.* standardbredcanada.ca/news/2-1-18/maiden-breaker-magical-albert.html.

Race Replay Videos

Woodbine Racetrack. (March 1, 2018). "Magical Albert" #6 claims victory and a new lifetime mark with Jonathan Drury aboard in Race #3, Woodbine Racetrack, Toronto, Retrieved from https://www.youtube.com/watch?v=czhV7uSQCSE

Woodbine Racetrack. (February 1, 2018). "Magical Albert" #6 claims his first lifetime win with Jonathan Drury aboard in Race #1, Woodbine Racetrack, Toronto, Retrieved from https://www.youtube.com/watch?v=9lbBmF1QaO8

Flamboro Downs. (November 2, 2016). "Mach Magic" #4 claims victory with Scott Coulter aboard in Race #9, Flamboro Downs, Dundas, Retrieved from http://www.flamborodowns.com/replays.html

Index

Index

H

Hamilton, 6, 19, 22, 81, 117, 199, 208, 226
Hamilton Public Library, 171
Hamm, Annette, 226-227
Hammond, Marie-Lynn, 258
Harley Z Tam (Nacho), 234-236, 242
Harrisburg, 95
Hayes, Darlene, 5-46, 54-80, 86-118, 135-142, 154, 158,
    161, 171, 180-181, 205-235, 243, 255-257
Hayes, Derrick, 5-46, 54-80, 86-141, 171, 180-181,
    210-212, 232, 236, 243, 256
Henderson, Shawna, 96, 97, 112, 132, 138
Henry, Trevor, 228
He's Watching, 2, 4, 142, 157, 181
Heza Big Dealer, 238
Hillsborough Stables, 5, 6, 14, 16-35, 40-46, 54-59, 64-80,
    86-87, 94, 99-109, 118-123, 134-142, 157, 167,
    180-184, 196, 233-244, 255-256, 258
Horse Canada, 193-194, 245

I

IAMSAM SAMIAM, 238
Indigo, 169, 187

J

Jamieson, Jody, 101
Johnston, Marg, 167

K

Keeneland, 26
Kern, Clint, 152-153
King, Stephen, 52

L

Larry's Petrock, 222-226

Renata Lumsden

O
Olliestrikesfame, 222
Ontario Veterinary College, 8, 17, 193, 236, 258
Ontario Writers' Conference, 56
Overlord, 219

P
Pharaoh, 203-204
Pontiac Luck, 64-65, 246
Porchak, Jeff, 201, 246
Portwood, Christie, 183-184
Prologue, 222-225, 228

Q
Queen Elizabeth Way, 18, 84

R

S
Sammy, 124
Sarasota Magic, 4, 30-32, 38-48, 50, 142, 132, 156
Sauble Ashley, 120-121
Shepherd, Robert, 155-156, 179
She's Magic, 2, 4, 142-143, 157, 176, 180, 204-216, 247, 256
Shorty Bones, 59-64, 87-88, 94-95, 102-118, 136-138, 157-158, 176, 182, 214, 240, 243, 256-257
Singh, Ranjit, 258
Slots at Racetrack Program (SARP), 19, 20, 59
So Raven, 101
Somebeachsomewhere, 3, 24-25, 30-31, 181, 231-233, 246
Some Lucky Magic, 4, 233, 241-242
Sports Cowboy, 204
Sports Expert, 120-121
Sports Tale, 219, 220, 222

Photograph Credits

Insert 1, page 1 (top left) Renata and Albert bond while a groom walks Lusi in the arena: Collection of Dave and Renata Lumsden

Insert 1, page 1 (top right) Renata bucket-feeding Albert: Collection of Dave and Renata Lumsden

Insert 1, page 1 (middle) Albert the neonatal foal struggles: image courtesy Dr. Luis G. Arroyo

Insert 1, page 1 (bottom left) Albert cocks his head every morning at Hillsborough Stables and lets out a welcome whinny: image courtesy Darlene Hayes

Insert 1, page 1 (bottom right) Lusi and Albert pause for a photo outside the barn before heading to the arena: Collection of Dave and Renata Lumsden

Insert 1, page 2 (top left) A close-up of Albert's lump: Collection of Dave and Renata Lumsden

Insert 1, page 2 (top right) Lusi and Albert share mare and foal paddock time together: Collection of Dave and Renata Lumsden

Insert 1, page 2 (middle) Pan and Shorty return to Hillsborough Stables: image courtesy Derrick Hayes

Insert 1, page 2 (bottom left) Dave feeds Lusi a peanut butter bar while Oscar watches: Collection of Dave and Renata Lumsden

Insert 1, page 2 (bottom right) The original wooden barn at Stonegate: Collection of Dave and Renata Lumsden

Insert 1, page 3 (top left) Lido and newborn She's Magic (Sheshe): image courtesy Darlene Hayes

Insert 1, page 3 (top right) Albert in the paddock at Classy Lane: image courtesy Lisa LeFort Beaton

Insert 1, page 3 (middle) Albert after ankle surgery: Collection of Dave and Renata Lumsden

Insert 1, page 4 (top) Lido and newborn Sara: image courtesy Darlene Hayes

Insert 1, page 4 (bottom) Dave and Lusi: Collection of Dave and Renata Lumsden

Insert 1, page 5 (top left) New barn and arena: Collection of Dave and Renata Lumsden

Insert 1, page 5 (top right) Albert sucking his tongue with mom Renata: Collection of Dave and Renata Lumsden

Insert 1, page 5 (middle) Tony training Albert: image courtesy Lisa LeFort Beaton

Insert 1, page 5 (lower left) Renata and Mach Magic: Collection of Dave and Renata Lumsden

Insert 1, page 5 (lower right) Pan and Shorty in the paddock beside the fieldstone house: image courtesy Darlene Hayes

Insert 1, page 6 (top) Lusi and Renata share paddock time together: Collection of Dave and Renata Lumsden

Insert 1, page 6 (middle) Renata and Albert: image courtesy Norm Files

Insert 1, page 6 (bottom) First meeting for Lusi and Nacho: image courtesy Darlene Hayes

Acknowledgements

To write the story of *Magical Albert*, I relied on the time, insights, and generosity of many wonderful people. Thank you to all those individuals connected to the harness-racing community in Ontario—from close friends to virtual strangers. Your love of horses and patience with my equine-related questions helped ensure authenticity and accuracy in the details. Much appreciation goes out to Debra Downing, Jean Moscardini, and Rebecca Williams for acting as all-important beta readers. Your combined comments strengthened the narrative and also narrowed down the number of photographs. Many thanks to Norm Files, Hillsborough Stables, Lisa Lefort Beaton, Ranjit Singh, the Ontario Veterinary College, and the University of Guelph for allowing the use of your photos and for lending your expertise to photo enhancement. I owe a huge debt of thanks to my friend and talented editor, Marie-Lynn Hammond, who brought the right mix of passion about writing, editing, and horses to the book. My gratitude goes out to Stephanie Fysh for fine-tuning the prose with her proofreading skills. Thank you to my parents for giving me the confidence to try and fail and try again in life. To Albert, his mother, Lusi, and all the other spirited Standardbred horses I've known, past and present, thank you for bringing so much joy and richness to my only go-round on this earth. To my husband, Dave—a very good man—thank you for your unwavering love and support and for always watching over our family and believing in all of us.